WHAT
MATTERS
MOST?

WHAT MATTERS MOST?

BRIAN DRAPER

LION

Published by Lion Books
an imprint of
Lion Hudson plc
Wilkinson House, Jordan Hill Road,
Oxford OX2 8DR, England
www.lionhudson.com/lion

ISBN 978 0 7459 5654 1
e-ISBN 978 0 7459 5656 6

First edition 2014

Acknowledgments

Scripture quotations taken from
the *Holy Bible, New International
Version*, copyright © 1973, 1978,
1984 International Bible Society.
Used by permission of Hodder &
Stoughton, a member of the Hodder
Headline Group. All rights reserved.
"NIV" is a trademark of International
Bible Society. UK trademark number
1448790.

p. 11: Extract taken from "To
That Which is Most Important"
by Anna Swir, from *Talking to My
Body*, translated by Czeslaw Milosz
and Leonard Nathan. Copyright
© 1996 by Czeslaw Milosz and
Leonard Nathan. Reprinted with
the permission of The Permissions
Company, Inc. on behalf of
Copper Canyon Press, www.
coppercanyonpress.org.

p. 38: Extract taken from
"Sometimes" by Sheenagh Pugh,
from *Selected Poems*, Seren, 1990.
Used by permission.

pp. 81, 110, 120: Extract taken
from *An Altar in the World* by
Barbara Brown Taylor, published by
Canterbuy Press, © 2009 Barbara
Brown Taylor. Used by permission.

p. 111: Extract taken from the song
"Let Yourself" by Martyn Joseph,
copyright © Martyn Joseph. Used by
permission.

p. 130: Extract taken from the song
"Ashes or Gold" by Miriam Jones,
copyright © Miriam Jones. Used by
permission.

A catalogue record for this book is
available from the British Library

Printed and bound in the UK,
September 2014, LH26

For Katharine,
my pure joy

Contents

Acknowledgments

I would like especially to thank John Moorhead for
helping to inspire the flow of this book through the
honesty and vibrancy of his own spiritual search,
which he's made from within – and yet never despite –
serious illness.

Beyond that, I am indebted to those who help me
to look for spiritual treasure within the ordinariness
of everyday life: a small community called the Order
of the Flower on the Pavement, which meets around
my kitchen table; Nick Chatrath and Alison Coulter
at Artesian, who are so much more than business
associates; all those who have shared their wisdom
within my Lent and Advent email series; my support
team led by Andrew Walsh and Rob Richards; Howard
Green, for his soulful sauntering and wisdom; Chris
and Sylvia Allison, who offered their shoulders just
when I needed help, and made so much possible; Dave
and Heather Pearson, for their generosity; Luke and
Jo Birmingham for their amazing hospitality; Chantal
Freeman for the lovely illustrations in this book; Ali Hull
for her patience and clarity as my editor; Katharine, my
rock; and Eden, Mercy, and Betsy-Joy, who have helped
me to unlearn most of what I thought I knew and to
remember more of What Matters Most in the end.

I thank God most of all for the love that courses
through the communities and networks, local and
global, of which I have been privileged to be part. For
without love…

Were I able to shut
my eyes, ears, legs, hands,
and walk into myself
for a thousand years,
perhaps I would reach –
I do not know its name –
what matters most.

(Anna Swir, "To That Which is Most Important")

Listen to your life. See it for the fathomless mystery it is. In the boredom and the pain of it, no less than in the excitement and gladness; touch, taste, smell your way to the holy and hidden heart of it.

(Frederick Buechner, from Now and Then: A Memoir of Vocation)

Give careful thought to your ways. You have planted much, but have harvested little. You eat, but never have enough. You drink, but never have your fill. You put on clothes, but are not warm. You earn wages, only to put them in a purse with holes in it.

(Haggai 1:5–6)

Introduction

Today I scheduled a morning run, before cracking on with the business of the day. There were chapters to write, people to see, calls to make, as there usually are. Halfway around my run, along a woodland path, I came across a woman who had fallen badly on her ankle and was howling with pain. (Turns out it was broken.) All thoughts of a schedule departed, as I tried to help this lady first to find more comfort, and then to contact her husband, and finally to help her back out along the woodland track.

I wasn't a hero or a Good Samaritan; you'd have done exactly the same thing. There are times when What Matters Most is clear; when the things we've worried about before the day has dawned pale into insignificance, compared with what the day brings us instead.

But sometimes life isn't as straightforward. It can be hard to know what really matters most, or what *should* matter when our days seem full of frustrating compromises and dissatisfying trade-offs. We have conflicting priorities, we find ourselves always at the beck and call of our "smart" technology, and it's hard to know what life is even meant to be about.

This book won't give you the straight answer to What Matters Most, because there isn't *one*. But it will give you space to regain perspective, and to engage your spiritual imagination. It will help you to develop some sustainable daily practices that will help to reveal more of the treasure hidden for us within ordinary life. And it will ask not only how to search creatively and tenaciously for What Matters Most – but to live as if you mean it.

A word about my spirituality

May I be clear from the start? My own reference points are Western and Christian, and I draw throughout this book from the contemplative tradition, whose great wisdom has helped me to make a more vibrant, relevant, and creative connection between "faith" and everyday life. But I am not a huge fan of religion, nor especially of religious jargon. In fact, I believe religious jargon is a barrier to people of all faiths and to those who wish to pursue more of What Matters Most for themselves. So in the following pages I'm looking to explore and express some of the most helpful points of connection between spirituality and everyday life, in a way that anyone could find accessible and welcoming, challenging and inspiring. At times, I'll include some of the distinctive contemplative elements of my own faith – such as a belief in God (though I will challenge us all to stay open to who and what God is), and an appreciation of the spiritual discipline of prayer (and how it can help us to become more open to *life* as a whole). As always, however, I have tried with all my heart to present any spiritual theme in a way that will inspire gentle curiosity, openness, and exploration.

Finding space – how to make the most of this book

It's hard to find space in our busy lives for the kind of serious (but accessible) reflection you'll find in this book. There are always more seemingly urgent tasks to complete, and so many of us struggle to give ourselves permission to stop.

It's like driving when you are lost. It's tempting to keep going, faster and faster, telling yourself you'll find the right road before long. But by pulling over to calm down, and to read the map, and to glimpse the bigger picture, you'll get back on track much more effectively.

So perhaps we could try something for a moment: four simple steps that you can practise anywhere, at any time.

Stop. Relax. Breathe. Smile.

You can take a few seconds to do this, or a few minutes, if you have longer. But if you practise these four steps *each time* you pick up this book, it will nurture a positive habit for you that will open up space within busyness-as-usual. You may not remember in ten years' time the specifics of what you have read here, but if you continue a habit – in this case, to stop, to relax, to breathe, and to smile – that's where you will make a lasting gain.

So try this now.

Stop. Simple as that! Create a firebreak between what you've just been doing and what you are about to do (which is to engage in reflection). Don't try to multitask. Just stop, and be. That's the first step. Do nothing, for a few moments, and notice what it's like.

And then…

Relax. Notice if there is any tension in your body – your forehead, your jaw, your shoulders, your back… the usual places where we store our stress physically! And try to relax your body. It's easier (and much more pleasant) to be present to the task in hand if you are relaxed. And it's amazing how we often don't even realize we are clenching our jaw or furrowing our brow until we stop to notice.

Breathe. We take too many shallow breaths when we are dashing breathlessly from place to place and task to task. So start to breathe a little more slowly and deeply. This is physically far better for us, a more efficient way of gaining energy from our breathing – but there's also the emotional benefit of calming down, the mental benefit of being present, and the spiritual benefit of becoming more centred.

Smile. Spiritual reflection is a serious thing, but that doesn't mean it has to be sombre. As you go, then, try to smile. A smile is joyfully infectious, after all – and throughout this book we are pursuing what is *good*. That means it's a joyfully positive process. There is no need to adopt the brace position. There are no nasty surprises here. It's all good. So remember to smile!

Looking for space
Just taking those four quick steps each time, before you start reading, will open up some space around you, and within you. Try it now, if you haven't already.

It's a crucial principle, to make space – not so that we may continue to do nothing, but so that we can act more decisively as a result. And the space is there to be discovered, if only we look. It's like the white space on this page behind the words. (The words would gain no definition without it.) It's like the silence from out of which a melody rises, and into which it falls once more. It's like the stillness between two waves of the sea, to borrow a phrase from T. S. Eliot. Stillness, space, and silence is essential in such a frenetic culture as ours, and you can *always* find it if you look for it.

As well as creating a simple rhythm of stopping, relaxing, breathing, and smiling as you read this book, you could also decide consciously *where* you will read it over the coming days, and find a space that is conducive to soulful reflection. A favourite chair, in a favourite room in your house. A park bench. Somewhere you love to go, for privacy or space to think. "Retreating" to such a place could help you to create a positive ritual, which factors in regular soul-time for yourself – and from which you will be able to draw deeply.

Finally, please don't rush. I have tried to break the book into short, accessible sections so that you can pause whenever you need to. Do use this as a chance to find a rhythm, to develop good habits, and to rediscover What Matters Most in the process.

Go well!

1

What Matters Most?

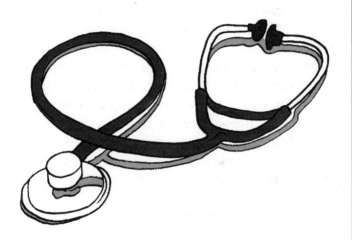

To what extent, I wonder, are we hurtling through life, pouring energy and money and time and most poignantly ourselves into things that may *not* matter, in the end? What a tragic waste that would be. The words of the Hebrew prophet Haggai, writing in the sixth century BC, seem to ring true for us today: most of us are working very hard to gain some kind of a better existence, but we don't seem to have much quality of life to show for it.

We're led to believe – by the culture, by the consumerist Western mindset, and in particular by our ego – that some things *really* do matter more than others, and should take priority. Yet all the while, our soul – if we stop to listen carefully – whispers back the question, ever so patiently, ever so quietly: "Yes: but what matters *most*?"

How much does it matter what other people think of me?

How much should it matter what they expect of me?

How much should it matter if my life doesn't work out as planned, predicted, or hoped?

It's tempting (and often easier) to pay attention to the seemingly urgent and short-term requirements of our egocentric worries than it is to the longer-term, gentler requirements of the soul. So we fret about things that almost always matter less in the long run than they seem to matter at the time. We compete fiercely against each other for trophies and trinkets that we know, in our heart of hearts, hardly matter a jot when set against the greater backdrop of more nobler causes. We let our relationships suffer, along with our peace of mind, and our sense of perspective, as we speed off unthinkingly in hot pursuit of what we unquestioningly *presume* matters most, because we see everyone else speeding off in the same direction ahead of us, and we fear being left behind.

If we didn't worry so much about the things we worry so much about, how much more time and energy would we have to dedicate to the question of the soul, to "What Matters Most" *in the end*?

Imagine what kind of difference it could make, day to day, if we lived by an alternative set of priorities, more co-operatively, creatively, and meaningfully – making a difference from within this stressful world we've all, in a sense, helped to create through our various anxious and insecure patterns of living. Because we simply can't go on the way we're going, can we? Locally or globally. Personally or communally.

The world is not in good shape: our generation faces unprecedented inequality between rich and poor, we're reaping the first fruits of climate change, we're struggling to find meaning beyond endless consumerism, and people are burning out through busyness. This isn't the kind of world I'd like to hand on to my children.

Though we may not change the whole world, we nevertheless have a profound opportunity to change the world around us, through waking up to what might matter most, and then living, like never before, as if it truly does.

*   *   *

But we need some help. We can't do it just with a pen and notebook and a few minutes set aside to reassess our priorities. It doesn't work like that (and anyway, an email or text will probably come in to distract us while we're trying!). We're not seeking a few "right" answers that can be plucked from thin air to solve our problems. Instead, we only discover What Matters Most when we set out practically to explore and express it for ourselves, through our very lives.

So throughout this book, we'll use some simple spiritual exercises that will help to open our eyes to a different way of being, as we start to see that what matters most is usually waiting to be discovered within the most ordinary and unsensational moments of everyday life. Treasure that we have missed, so far, because we were looking so hard over there for something that was *here*, all along.

Simple, Good, and Lasting

Frequently (although not always), it's the people who are nearing the end of their lives who are liberated most demonstrably from the preoccupations and distractions of their ego, to discover more clearly What Matters Most. And it's worth paying attention to what such people end up valuing, as they are pioneers – people who go before us, along a path we know we will have to walk ourselves some day.

A friend of mine, John, recently wrote to tell me that his cancer had returned, aggressively, and that he had chosen, after very careful thought, to stop his chemotherapy treatment.

Yet hear his words:

"Although grieving for others who will deal with my absence, I nevertheless experience strong waves of the anticipation of good. That good will simply be a deeper experience of the joy I have now, in the kiss of the wind on my cheek, the cool, soft grass comforting my feet, the pink and purple skies changing by the minute, the sound of a child laughing or an ocean roar, or the taste of my wife's lips.

"Perhaps, more than any of these, though," he concludes, "is the deep joy in receiving love, even as I pass it on."

Real words, from a real man who is experiencing "strong waves of the anticipation of good", despite the prognosis being really bad. I hope you find them as moving and inspirational as I do. There are three very powerful things to notice here, in particular, which will help us to narrow our own search for What Matters Most.

First, there is the *clarity and simplicity* of sensing, in the end, What Matters Most (though this won't be the same list for everyone). For John, it's the kiss of the wind, the feel of the grass, the sound of a child laughing, the taste of lips... And such clarity is contagious. It makes me want to stop worrying about so much of the ephemera of life – where the next pay cheque is coming from, how my Twitter account is growing, whether the car will keep going for another year – and go outside and feel the kiss of the wind, too, because I know what it means to this man, and I see its worth, and it resonates with my soul.

I know that the process of discovering What Matters Most wasn't simple or filled with clarity for John, who has not led an easy life. But what he's come to appreciate *is* clear and simple. Perhaps you, like me, envy his clarity, if not his circumstance.

Second, What Matters Most to John is also what is discernibly *good*. It's important to remember this, as we pause to reflect for ourselves. While the ego is likely to drive us "onward and upward", relentlessly, through feelings of insecurity, fear, and the need to control, compete, and compare – our soul, instead, is tuned into a different set of values, and will guide us gently but inexorably, if we let it, toward that which is good.

Third, John senses that What Matters Most will last beyond his physical life – and not only that, but will become an ever deeper experience of "the joy I have now". What hope! In other words, there is a trajectory to life that takes us into death, crucially, and then beyond it. And some aspects of our experience, as John says, will deepen, and some things will last. More than anything, he admits, this is all to do with love: the love we receive, and the love we pass on.

It's painfully simple wisdom, gained not so much through sitting in a library (though John loves his theology) as from getting within the crucible of everyday living. And given the choice – between committing to what will not, ultimately, matter, or to what will – I know what I'd prefer to submit the rest of my own life to.

* * *

Je ne regrette rien

Why wait, after all, to discover the simplicity
and clarity, the goodness, and the lasting, loving
fruitfulness of What Matters Most?

The point is not only to discover but to *live*
within such a reality, here and now. But if we
speed on without pausing to reflect on the nature
of our lives as we go – or if we simply keep telling
ourselves that "one day" we'll give ourselves the
space to attend to the really significant stuff of life
– then sadly we are likely to end up with regrets.
And who wants those?

Bronnie Ware is a former palliative care nurse
in Australia who noticed, over several years of
looking after people in the final days of their lives,
that they expressed similar themes in terms of
their regrets, or what they would do differently
given a second shot at life. These included "being
more genuine, not working so hard, expressing
one's true feelings, staying in touch with friends,
and finding more joy in life". How intriguing.
Perhaps more than one of those themes resonates
with you.

When it comes to being more genuine, many
of us are still trying to live up to the expectations
of our parents or teachers or people who were
in authority over us when we were younger.
Sometimes we continue trying to please them,
even when they are no longer alive. And we can
live much of our lives unthinkingly trying to
please others, by doing what we think they expect,
instead of courageously pursuing a different
path. Let's remember that we're often guessing or

presuming what other people expect of us, too – when the reality may be very different.

The theme of working too hard is a difficult one. Hard work is a good thing, of course – and we can't just drop out and head to the beach whenever we fancy it. And yet... How many of us work far longer than we need to, because we are afraid of being spotted going home on time, for example, when everyone else is working late to impress each other? How many of us could achieve more in less time, with better focused ways of working, higher quality breaks in between our work (such as eating lunch, away from a desk!), and the common sense to know when enough is really enough?

A third regretful theme, of not expressing one's true feelings, is a real wake-up call, especially if you're a people-pleaser like me. It's too easy to suppress our feelings in order to keep the peace with those around us. But if we do, we can end up living someone else's life instead.

Then there's staying in touch with friends. Friendship is often the first thing to suffer when we work too hard. But it's easy to let friendships slip for any number of reasons. There are some people out there who know us deeply, and who love us, and who are very good for us, just as we are good for them. It mattered to many of the people who spoke to Bronnie Ware that they had let their deepest friendships drift.

And then finally there's the question of finding more joy in life. As we grow older, it's very easy to cover over that childlike sense of playfulness and freedom we used to enjoy. For all sorts of reasons, we can become over-earnest, task-focused and fear-driven. Yet life is a gift!

So why not look for the joy within it, whenever we can? The challenge is to learn to live with greater freedom *now*, and perhaps, most importantly, to give ourselves permission to savour and enjoy life, whatever our circumstances.

*   *   *

If you have time, pause for a few moments now, to write your own short list of the regrets you could be left with if you were to carry on without making any proactive changes to your lifestyle. Once you have done that, ask yourself:

What would I do differently if I were given a second shot at the life I have already lived? And what first step would I need to take to start living as if this *were* my second chance?

Now, take that step.

Where to look?
I was chatting with a friend once about the big questions of life. He said he'd been on a road trip across the United States, in search of some answers to those big questions. The trouble is, he said, he came back with more questions than he started with. So he decided that the only thing left, in the end, was to keep living at such a fast pace that one day, somewhere along the way, he might bump into some of the answers for himself.

I love his desire to find those answers. But what if the search were less "out there" and more "in here", *within* us? The spiritual search doesn't have to involve covering as much ground as possible in the shortest time available, or accumulating more ideas or possessions or experience; instead it will turn us inside out, if we let it, as we journey inward toward the very heart of life itself.

As such, the exercises and reflections in this book will remind us – and we all need reminding, daily – that the most significant journey we can take is within, into the hidden depths of who we are. But don't worry: this is no esoteric exercise in navel-gazing. As we explore ever more deeply inside ourselves, to discover more of What Matters Most to us, we cannot help but express that journey outwardly through our everyday actions: through this one life we are called to live, and to give. Our "being" is linked intrinsically to our "doing", and we cannot have one without the other. So as we reflect inwardly about who we are and what is important to us, we will make a difference outwardly through our creative and practical response.

We will not find the right answer, therefore, awaiting us on the final page of this book, or sealed in a golden envelope with our name on it. Instead, it's through the very process of exploring inwardly and expressing outwardly that we will discover more, for ourselves, of What Matters Most in the end.

*　　*　　*

Another short exercise

If you were to take an inventory of what you own, and how you spend your time each day, I wonder what it would tell you about your current priorities?

Spend a few moments now, sketching out one of your typical days on a piece of paper. Try not to judge yourself against a hypothetical right answer to "what matters most", but just be honest with yourself about what's been attracting your time and attention.

You might like to spend a few minutes walking around your house, noticing what you have, and what you don't have. What takes pride of place? What has been hidden away, or neglected? What stories do your possessions tell about who you are and what's important to you?

Perhaps doing this quick inventory may surprise you. Try to see it through the eyes of a complete stranger from another culture, and imagine what they might deduce from watching a typical day or week in your life, and from what you've accumulated.

What would you like to keep?

What would you like to change?

* * *

It's quite possible there's a gap between the way you've ended up living, day to day, and what you are already beginning to *sense* deeper down really matters most to you (even if you can't fully articulate it yet). Because there's a gap for all of us, if we're honest. I know there is for me. You may simply have lost touch with yourself over the last few years of raising children or working hard; you may have been preoccupied with seemingly urgent short-term tasks (which never seem to end!), or you may just be worn out or feel that you have lost your way.

But as we go in search of What Matters Most, the good news is that we don't need to go too far before we begin to spot some of the things that were there all along, which we couldn't see for looking. The things that we might take for granted, perhaps, usually until such a time as we're about to lose them.

It helps us to reflect on those things *now*, because the simplest things we appreciate are sometimes so familiar that we can't see them; yet in looking, finding and celebrating them, we begin to see more of who we were truly created to be, as well.

2

Keep it simple,
pursue goodness,
and it will last!

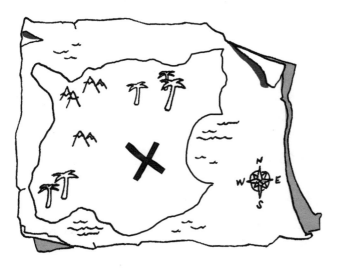

I'd like to take us back to John's brief description – facing, as he is, such an uncertain future – of What Matters Most to him, because he has come to appreciate what's **simple**, **good**, **lasting,** and **loving** with searing clarity. We'll leave the matter of love until the final chapter of this book, but let's pause now to consider those first three principles a little more closely – simple, good, and lasting – because they will encourage us not to overcomplicate things as we go.

Simple is as simple does

It's tempting to make life more complex than it really needs to be, isn't it? That's perhaps because we remain fearful deep down that we'll look foolish or stupid in front of the rest of the class if we dare to keep it simple. Remember the essays you wrote at college? You probably tried to make them sound more clever than they needed to be, to impress your tutor, or even yourself. Life sometimes feels like it should be harder to work out, like an opaque poem, and that it should be a struggle to come to any deeper understanding of what it's really all about.

That's not to deny the beauty and complexity of the many and varied ecosystems within life, the universe, and everything... But when it comes to the way we live, and to what we believe, and (especially) what matters to us in the end, there's a pressure to think that nothing could ever be that simple. The wind blowing in your face? *Really*? The sound of a child laughing...?

Yet St Paul wrote a letter to the church in Corinth in which he said, "God chose the foolish things of the world to shame the wise; God chose the weak things of the world to shame the strong" (1 Corinthians 1:27). It's a stumbling block of a spiritual principle: that the secret to life is not hidden away in the most complex philosophies or esoteric theories, but in plain sight, for the eyes of those people who are often overlooked themselves or considered insignificant.

When we try to be too clever about it, we can look straight past the ordinary, in search of the extraordinary, and miss What Matters Most in the process. We might be working all hours God sends us in order to give our children the very best start in life, when what they really need is more of the simple presence of a father or mother. We might be so obsessed by reading the latest theological theories that we forget to practise what we believe. We might be so focused on solving what's going wrong with the world that we miss the chance to demonstrate in day-to-day life what can be right.

* * *

Simple wisdom

The activist and author Shane Claiborne learned first-hand from Mother Teresa how to put his faith into practise imaginatively and vividly. He established an inspiring community called the Simple Way in inner-city Philadelphia, and at the turn of 2013 he made a series of thirteen new-year resolutions for himself, which he shared online (http://www.redletterchristians.org/13-hopes-for-2013/). This is someone who gets things done by keeping it simple. But let's remember, as we read a few of them now, that simple does not necessarily mean easy. To simplify is to distil the essence of something, in order to get to the heart of What Matters Most. It takes great nerve thereafter to live by a simple code.

"Give more money away than I keep," he writes, "and do it in a way that takes away the power of money and celebrates the power of love." Ouch. There's not much room there for complex tax arrangements in order to bend the rules and maximize our returns. There's no room for selfishness. He knows exactly where he stands, month by month, according to his own economy, which flies in the face of contemporary unfettered capitalism. (These resolutions are not for everyone, of course – they are simple principles he has decided to live by. You and I have to consider our own.)

"Compliment someone I have a hard time complimenting… and mean it," he writes.

"Pause before every potential crisis and ask: 'Will this matter in five years?'" (This really works. I have tried it.)

So you might identify one of these to try, as an exercise in refining What Matters Most *to you*. Otherwise, ask yourself how your own wisdom could be distilled into distinctive resolutions, or guidelines for life, which you could express simply and effectively. And then start writing your own list.

Here's another, in the meantime, for those of us who long to live more imaginatively and courageously, but never know quite where to start:

"Do for *one person*," he writes, "what I wish I could do for everyone, but can't." Simple.

* * *

Another example of someone keeping their wisdom very simple is the columnist and author Regina Brett. When she turned forty-five, she wrote down forty-five lessons that she had learned in life. They soon circulated widely, as people were drawn to the clarity of the wisdom she espoused.

"4. *Don't take yourself so seriously. No one else does.*

"20. *When it comes to going after what you love in life, don't take no for an answer.*

"37. *Your children get only one childhood. Make it memorable.*"

Perhaps someone has passed some wisdom on to you, from down the generations, that you have appreciated, and will also pass on. If there is one thing you've been told by a parent or grandparent, or an older, wiser figure that has stayed with you, what is it?

Sadly, sometimes, the wisdom or advice isn't always there. The sages in our community are diminishing, as society is increasingly fragmented and we dispatch our elderly, once the gatekeepers of wisdom, to their care homes. If there was one piece of advice you wish you had been given earlier in life but weren't, what is it?

Simple prayer

Simplicity can also extend to more overtly "spiritual" acts such as prayer, which we tend to overcomplicate if we're not careful. St Francis kept it very simple when he prayed. Famously, he would stay up all night praying: "Who are you, O God; and God, who am I?" He knew what mattered most when it came to the subject of his prayers. In staying with something as simple as a prayer like this, we can begin to find hidden depths, many layers, textures, and nuances. Instead of wasting our time and energy verbalizing lists of wants, a prayerful focus on something as "simple" as our own identity and God's can yield a depth and power to our contemplative life that we hardly knew was there at all.

A singular focus

The people who get things done are usually the people, like Shane Claiborne, who have a simple and singular focus in life. In today's culture, we like to think we can multitask like crazy and we wear busyness as a badge of honour, complaining and boasting in equal measure about how many balls we have to keep in the air, or how many plates we are currently spinning. But the leadership expert Tony Schwartz warns very strongly that there is no such thing as "multitasking". "A growing body of research," he writes, "suggests that we're most productive when we move between periods of *high-focus* and intermittent rest." In other words, when we spend short bursts of time doing one thing, and one thing only – before resting and recharging.

The trouble is, most of us don't inhabit such a simple rhythm. "Instead," he laments, "we live in a grey zone, constantly juggling activities but rarely engaging in any of them – or fully disengaging from any of them. The consequence is that we settle for a pale version of the possible."

The problem of good

Let's turn to our second principle now: goodness. It's hugely underrated, and grossly neglected in Western culture, where our background sense of fear and suspicion flows nightly from the news channels and keeps us inwardly braced for trouble. Our focus, as a culture, is almost entirely on what is wrong with the world. But if we were to look, instead, for what is right, and what is good, then the way we see the world can change dramatically.

*　　*　　*

I love that opening scene from the film Love Actually, with its monologue from Prime Minister Hugh Grant, set to a moving sequence involving pictures of ordinary people greeting one another at the airport. Whenever he gets gloomy with the state of the world, he says, he thinks about the arrivals gate at Heathrow, where people are waiting to welcome back their loved ones with hugs and kisses – husbands, wives, mothers, fathers, sons, daughters, boyfriends, girlfriends, old friends... It's not a spectacular or newsworthy kind of love, but it's real, and present, and all around us, if only we are willing to see it.

I don't know about you, but for some reason I grew up believing that the world was going to hell in a handcart. Standards were slipping. Crime was rising. The kids had no respect. "Things aren't what they used to be" seemed to be the constant refrain. We were schooled to believe that the world was becoming a nastier place in which to live. I suppose you only had to catch the headlines a few times to start believing this was true.

The trouble is, this kind of thinking can become an endlessly self-fulfilling prophecy: so that if we keep looking for what's bad, and what's worse, we *will* keep finding it – and in the process we'll reinforce the pessimistic belief that we don't stand a chance of making a difference to this world, so why bother?

Perhaps it's just simpler to look for the bad. Perhaps we fear the disappointment too much of going after the good and never finding it.

But what if the naysayers were wrong? What if the world wasn't such a bad place after all? What if it were quite the opposite – positively alive, like a spring morning, with possibility, with promise, with potential? Of course, the systems we have created – of consumption and production – may be twisted, unfair, unjust. That is a different matter. But the universe itself, and God's creation, and people, at their best: these are good.

What if the world were the sort of magical place in which we, too, were waiting to burst into life, as part of Eden's garden, as part of the beauty of the place itself, as part of its unstoppable energy?

And what if this world were the sort of place in which every single one of us really did have a potent choice: to resign ourselves to a pale version of the possible, as Tony Schwartz says, or to *become* the difference and thus to embody life itself?

In his book *Immortal Diamond* the Franciscan priest Richard Rohr suggests: "We have to be taught how to look for anything infinite, positive or good, which for some reason is more difficult." We struggle to see it – but that doesn't mean it's not there.

"We have spent centuries of philosophy trying to solve 'the problem of evil'," he continues, "yet I believe the much more confounding and astounding issue is 'the problem of good'. How do we account for so much gratuitous and sheer goodness in this world? Tackling this problem would achieve much better results."

"The problem of good." Now *there*'s a phrase! I wonder how much good has touched your life, without you hardly noticing, recently. If you were to stop, to reflect, now, on how much goodness has been gently but actively breaking out around you, despite your challenging or difficult circumstances, what kind of list could you make?

Spend a few moments writing or reflecting upon two or three good things that have happened recently, that you may have forgotten about. Why not respond by writing a note to someone who has brought goodness into your life?

* * *

And now, before we continue, let's get one thing absolutely clear.

When we talk about goodness, we don't mean

a foolish act of denial – a "glass half-full" kind of naïve optimism in which we refuse to see the reality of our situation, sticking our heads in the sand like ostriches to pretend everything is OK when it's not. Our problems won't go away just by ignoring them like a final reminder for a bill we can't ever hope to pay.

There *is* darkness in this world, plenty of it, and it comes in many forms: we might simply feel like we're stumbling around in the gloom, unsure of where to go next in life; we might feel the creeping darkness of depression or anxiety; we may have experienced the pitch blackness of personal tragedy, in which our world fell in on us and left us buried in the rubble of despair.

Darkness *is* real. And few, if any, of us need convincing otherwise. We believe in the darkness, we sense its grip, we fear what it brings. Yet here's the thing: just as the darkness is real, *so too is the light.* It's just far harder, sometimes, to believe in it; to believe that the good will out, that we can live in hope, that all will be well.

The prophets of old knew all about the darkness, but they refused to be overcome by it. "Darkness covers the earth, and thick darkness is over the peoples," wrote the prophet Isaiah (60:2), around 700 BC. Yet his words and his life pointed ultimately not to the darkness around him, but to what would emerge from it: "Arise, shine," he declared, "for your light has come!" (60:1). Arise. Shine.

*   *   *

"Stuff happens" in life, as the saying goes. It always does. We know that. But good stuff happens too. As the poet Sheenagh Pugh writes,

> *Sometimes things don't go, after all,*
> *from bad to worse.*

Sometimes, all *does* go well. We might move house and find a vibrant new community to become part of, never looking back. A friend of ours might get better from an illness. We might land an engaging and fulfilling job, at last – one that really, truly satisfies us. Our best-laid plans might succeed. Our prayers might even be answered. It could happen. It *does* happen.

But we find it harder to accept that the good stuff can happen to us, or even that it *has* happened to us. And for some reason, we often have to look harder for the good, even if it's been sitting there right before our eyes all along. (Sometimes we choose deliberately not to see the good around us, for all sorts of reasons.)

Yet seek, and you will find, as Jesus once said. The question is, what are we seeking? Because this really does have a profound effect on the way we see the world...

... and the way we see the world has a profound effect on the way we are...

... and the way we are has a profound effect on the world around us.

So our own seeking, our own search, has the potential to become highly contagious. Transformed people can transform other people.

* * *

Let's take a practical example, and think for a moment about the way you end your day. For many of us, the last thing we watch before we go to bed is the news. We catch the headlines, but then try to sleep with our minds and hearts stuffed with a litany of what's gone wrong today. (It *is* important to watch the news, of course: in order to make a difference, and to become part of the solution, we need to know what needs challenging, and who needs helping. But we don't necessarily need to let the news agenda have the final word.)

What if we tried, instead, to remember and be thankful for some of the good things that have happened to us or to people we know – good things that are in danger of slipping past us unnoticed or forgotten? Think of those glimmers in the darkness that have brought light and life: the laughter we shared with a friend; the helping hand we received from a stranger; the sound of the sea on a windy afternoon's walk; the cold drink we enjoyed on a hot, thirsty day; the thank you we received from our boss for the good work we'd done.

Such simple goodness has the power to restore, to bring energy, to bring us back to life. It's all there, and it's all real. It's just that we tend without thinking to discount the positive, in search of the negative.

To switch this search around can take great courage and will, as the Polish psychologist Andrew Bienkowski suggests. Courage, he writes, is "the conscious act of refusing to live in fear". "And sometimes," continues the man who was exiled to Siberia with his family after the Second World War, and who lost everything in the process, "it is actively searching for hope. Even in the bleakest of circumstances, if we can find but a small spark of hope, we can nurture it, feed it until it becomes a great fire of determination."

Made to last?

The third principle of What Matters Most to consider is whether or not something is lasting.

Nothing seems to last forever, especially in our disposable culture. We buy things, but if they break or need updating, we throw them away. Few consumer durables are built for life as they once were.

Usually, however, when we have lived for long enough that we can look back some distance, we gain a clearer idea of what's of lasting worth to us. Usually it's not the physical things we buy, however valuable they may be; instead, it's their associations with certain times, or with people who may have moved on. If you ask someone what they'd save first if their house were burning down (aside from the people and pets, of course), it's often photos – because they prompt most clearly the memories of experiences that have mattered so much that they have become a part of us, and have helped to shape and form us.

Looking back, what has stayed with you most powerfully, in a positive way – a memory, an association, a memento or experience that matters so much that it's of truly lasting worth to you? And what do you think is the essence of this, that you carry, into the present, and will take with you into the future?

Do not store up for yourselves treasures on earth, where moths and rust destroy, and where thieves break in and steal. But store up for yourselves treasures in heaven, where moths and rust do not destroy, and where thieves do not break in and steal. For where your treasure is, there your heart will be also.

(Matthew 6:19–21)

An associated question concerns what we may have already done that has lasting consequences. More often than not, while you may have made an impact on the physical world around you (in the way that a builder or architect may have left buildings, or a gardener may have shaped landscapes), the main difference you will have made is to people. And what they carry positively with them, of your own contribution, they are likely to treasure.

Maya Angelou said, "I've learned that people will forget what you said, people will forget what you did, but people will never forget how you made them feel." I wonder what you leave people with, and how you leave them feeling?

Jesus warned us not to store up treasure on earth that can be destroyed or stolen, but to store up treasures "in heaven". It's easy to presume that he was talking about performing good deeds here on Earth in order to get a reward once you've passed through the pearly gates and into the next life. In fact, he said that the kingdom of heaven was (and still is) close at hand, and emphasized that this kingdom is "within you" (Luke 17:21). Treasures in heaven are therefore not pie in the sky when you die; they have an "earthly" value – albeit a different kind of value, for a different kind of treasure.

What have you done, in your life, that other people will treasure so deeply in their own hearts, in that sacred, inner place where neither rust nor moth will destroy? What treasure have you deposited there for them, that will outlast the sagging of their skin and the tarnishing of the shiny surface of their lives?

Many of us would probably love to make our mark more famously on the world. If you're a musician, you may wish you could leave a classic album so that you'll always be remembered. If you're a writer, you want to leave a bestselling book! But most of us won't have a statue or a place in the history books to keep our name alive; it's likely that our greatest legacy will in fact be the way we've touched others when it has mattered most to them, in a way that's simple, good, and lasting. And this is far more precious, and of infinitely greater worth, than any kind of fame.

How would someone speak of you at your funeral? It's easy to look back on what we've done and think we haven't measured up to the standards of the world. We haven't competed well, or we haven't come first. We may not leave a large financial inheritance to our children. But the truth is you *will* have deposited plenty of treasure already.

* * *

What will go with you beyond this life?

It's deeply touching to read that John believes his experience of the kiss of the wind, the cool soft grass, the pink and purple skies, the sound of an ocean roar, the taste of his wife's lips – his experience of all of this will only be deepened.

It's an old cliché that we can't take anything with us when we die. Certainly, we can't pack a physical suitcase and stash our diamond rings or our share certificates. But the kingdom of heaven is a place that transcends time and space. It finds a home in the physical, visible world of the here and now, deep within us; yet it's John's great hope, and mine, too, that when we die, the hospitality is beautifully reciprocated; that we will then most fully find *our* home deep within the kingdom of heaven.

And so, in a sense, we are able to plan for a future that is rooted in the here and now, because we can store treasure in heaven, which lasts, and will be there waiting for us. The things that truly mattered most, which touched our heart, which stirred our soul, which we received from others, and which we have passed on in love. This is treasure worth seeking! The treasure we can both give and receive, and that endures forever.

So, three principles to help us narrow the focus as we search for What Matters Most. **Keep it simple, pursue goodness, and it will last.**

3

How do we matter?

Sometimes we might think we don't matter at all. Sometimes we might think we matter more than we do. But life is not a competition, nor an exercise in endless comparison with others. So rather than asking whether or not we matter, it's instead worth asking *how*.

Saying that, it's almost impossible to engage in self-reflection without getting entangled in the myriad insecure and anxious thoughts that seem to stream through our minds – about what makes us matter, and why, and how.

It's my ego that creates the running commentary in my head, which I find so hard to switch off, and which works overtime to create and bolster a sense of identity for me, from all of the things I've achieved and bought and done in my life. The ego tends to be insecure, and its raison d'être is to prove that we matter – but in so doing, it pushes us onward to *do* more in order to achieve more and thus somehow to demonstrate that we *are* more.

And that running commentary can get very confusing.

Do I matter more because I came top of the class?

Do I matter less because I was never picked for the team?

Do I matter more because I got the promotion and the bigger house?

Do I matter less because I didn't have children?

We can be caught in an endless cycle of fearful conjecture about what we need to do in order to matter more or most in the eyes of the world, and also in our own eyes. And unfortunately, there is always more that can be done to prove, or improve upon, this sense of worth, and so we keep on trying. It can be tiring and bewildering in equal measure, and we can end up spending much or most of our lives trying to demonstrate to whoever wants to watch that we do or did matter.

The wonderful thing is, however, that when it comes to how and why we matter, some of the times we mattered most are also the times when there was *nothing we could do...* but simply to "be there" for somebody. And this is very good news indeed.

*   *   *

Now, if you find this hard to believe, just think about a time when someone was there for *you*.

Cast your mind back to when you were experiencing a painfully hard season. Perhaps you were bereaved, or you had lost a job, or your relationship was breaking up, or you'd been told you were seriously ill. Sadly, we have all endured such difficult times, to a varying degree or other.

But happily, for most of us at least, there was somebody around who could help us – not that they probably felt that they *were* helping in the slightest at the time. In fact, they may have felt useless. Nevertheless, in simply "being there", it's likely that the friend or family member who sat with you did far more than they realized.

*   *   *

Ironically, when we arrive at that point of helplessness – where there is nothing we can do but "be there" for someone – it's perhaps the point at which we are able most strongly to be who we truly are. For we find ourselves released, for a short while, from the ego's impulse to prove our worth, to add our value, and instead we are able to provide someone with the greatest gift we can really offer, which is our full presence.

I wonder, when was the last time you gave someone the gift of your full and true presence? It's not easy in today's world, when there is always a phone or a screen close by to distract you. I watched two ladies having a conversation at the airport recently, and one simply couldn't stop looking at her phone as she chatted. She was there physically, but not mentally or spiritually!

But think back to the time you *were* there for someone, when you put the phone down, and the rest of the world seemed to fade into the background, and you were "there" palpably in a way that went beyond doing something for them to being present with them instead.

I remember responding once to a friend's call for help. He was struggling with some profound issues in his life – relationships, career, faith – and felt quite urgently lost in a fog. I jumped in the car and drove a long way to see him. When I arrived, I felt as though I had to justify my journey and prove my worth to him as some kind of wise counsellor – as if – and so I set about trying to advise him, even fix him and his "problems".

We got nowhere, fast, of course. It was only when I ceased my striving, and began instead to just be there, that my friend found the space to speak and to process a few things for himself… And by the end of the evening, he was able to articulate very powerfully what mattered most to him, and our meeting became a helpful way-marker along that part of his lifelong journey.

In the process, I had noticed something powerful about my own presence: that it was, indeed, a gift of true worth, as long as I didn't feel the need to disguise it with a mask of worthiness or utility.

The being *is* the doing

This is something of a mystery, certainly. But in the process of letting be, and being there, we are able not just to give ourselves to others in a profound and transformational way, but we are also able to see – sometimes for the first time – the goodness of the presence that flows through us to the world around us.

It is a counter-intuitive thing to do, however, to cease our striving and to be there, in the bare simplicity of who we really are. It takes courage not to try to fix or prove our worth or to feel we must always add some kind of demonstrable value. But this is the nature of everyday spirituality – there is usually a sense of a twist, an upside-down and inside-out feeling to what is unfolding in us and through us.

So we have to change the way we see things. In this instance, being present is not passive, about doing nothing. It is dynamic, active – proactive, even. To be fully with someone, we have to lay down our egos, and banish distractions, and be attentive, and sink deeply into the space that they inhabit. It is not for the faint-hearted. But as we do, we are more fully able to seek the spiritual treasure of a shared moment in time, a communion, a connection that has the power to transform.

*　　*　　*

Such true presence is positively contagious, by the way, and here is yet more spiritual treasure simply waiting to be discovered.

Think of someone you know who seems to have a seriously positive and inspiring presence about them; they probably seem to be less hurried, more assured, more attentive, and open, and *here*.

And that's because they are present – to you, to life, to the moment that lies before them. They are not distracted, or too busy, or thinking about themselves obsessively. They have nurtured presence and are able to challenge and inspire those around them *as much through who they are* as through what they do. So you might feel your soul stirring when you meet them. You could feel more alive. And you could feel inspired, just by being around them, to be more fully alive to the possibilities of the present moment yourself.

You won't find these rare people always telling you what you need to know, or what you need to do, but instead somehow inspiring you to search yourself for What Matters Most.

Your presence, then, is not only powerfully helpful to people who are undergoing crisis or who need someone simply to be there for them. When you allow yourself to "be there", wherever you find yourself, the very goodness of your presence will touch those around you, and help them to become aware of their own. *You simply cannot help it.* You pass something on that is contagious in a positively good way, without having to strive or to force anything upon anyone.

No wonder the poet Rainer Maria Rilke said, "Being here is so much." It takes courage to be here and to be present to others, but when we manage it, the being *is* the doing. It is a flow between two people, a rippling out of what is simple, good, and lasting, which in turn can flow through them to others, too.

*   *   *

Being open to others

One very simple way to strengthen your presence is simply to *practise* being fully present to other people. You might decide that for a whole day, you will do just that: try to be present. Or perhaps for just a morning. Or you might even decide simply to start with being present for one conversation or meeting.

But here's something you could do, which is based on a form of contemplation that we'll come on to more fully later. When you are with someone, this can be your spiritual practice or discipline.

Make your intention to be fully open to them – to what they have to say, to how they are, and to who they are. This means that you are not there to get your own point across, or to impress, or to dominate. Instead, your intention is to be there (of course, there will be times when they are there for you, and you are both there for each other).

But this time, be there, with them, for them. And here's the challenge: during your time with them, thoughts will inevitably distract you (you wouldn't be human if they didn't), dragging you away from the present, back into the past or forward into the future, or else luring you toward your to-do list. Anywhere, really. The human mind is restless, and won't let us settle very easily into the present; yet the present is where we experience times of creative insight, personal transformation, deep empathy for others, and, of course, presence.

So here's a trick. Whenever you become conscious that you are thinking, and that this thinking is taking you away from being open and present to the person you're with, use a special word – such as "open", or "present", or "be", or "here", or something similar – to alert you to the fact that you have drifted away, and to help to bring you straight back to the moment, to a place of openness and presence.

Keep the same word – don't vary it, unless you decide specifically that it's not helpful. And when you speak it (inwardly!), let go of what you were thinking about. Stop the train of thought, as it were, and disembark. This is crucial, as it helps you to develop the art of letting go; the gesture, if you like, of release.

Why does this help? Well, we are so quick to make assumptions, about things people say, or about situations, or about people, and these assumptions are frequently wrong. We are so quick to make judgments, which cloud our objectivity within any situation. We are so quick to offer solutions, which are *our* solutions, and not necessarily what your friend or colleague or family member needs to hear.

If you practise being open, and letting go of the thoughts that distract and entangle your mind, you will find yourself more fully present in many ways.

If what they say triggers a story of your own, try to let it go. You'll be tempted to jump in with those famous words, "Oh, that reminds me…" Instead, speak your word inwardly, and return to being open, listening fully, being there.

If what they say sparks the judgmental side in you – and this is the really testing part – try to resist thinking any the less of them, or differently about them, or patronizingly about them – and instead, once again, let them be.

And if what they say or do makes you want to try, somehow, to fix them or their problems, then instead let your full presence provide space for them to reflect for themselves on their situation, and perhaps to feel the goodness of your presence and to find strength in their own.

It's a mystery, this process, but it's not nebulous. It really does make a difference. Remember, we have to work hard to keep it simple, because our ego and our overactive, insecure minds will want to prove our worth to the watching world and to overcomplicate things. But the simplicity of "being there" is the most powerful start you can make along this journey, and it is worth practising daily from here to eternity.

*   *   *

Beyond such openness, we can also begin to discard the assumptions and mental representations we hold about other people. For unless we are willing to surrender what we *think we know* about someone, especially someone we intend to love, then we will only ever engage with the image or impression we have of that person, instead of the real person behind the image.

As Pope Francis says, reality is more important than our *ideas* about reality. "Realities simply are, whereas ideas are worked out," he says. Ideas are "conceptual elaborations" that cloud the way we see. What stops us from seeing more clearly is, in a sense, the way we have become used to seeing – based on previously held ideas, opinions, preconceptions about (in this case) other people. Our vision becomes blurred by what we believe we know about them instead of sharpened by what we do not know.

We might also, if we dare, apply such a principle to ourselves.

Open to yourself

The mystery of just "being there" for others helps us to discover more of the treasure of presence that we can almost unknowingly offer them. But once we have become aware of the goodness of our own presence, our journey of self-discovery can take an exciting turn.

Sometimes it can feel self-indulgent to think about ourselves. But it's important to know who we are, and the uniqueness that we bring to the world, in order to be more assured as we go.

It's only when we don't know who we are that we try too hard, and seek to impress others and establish our place in the hierarchy and order of things. The trouble is, this is ego-driven, and usually takes us away from the truth of our identity. We end up covering over our soulful or "true" self, masking it with poses and roles that we think will impress others and "establish" ourselves in the process.

The truth is, once we have begun to experience the gentle goodness of our own presence, there is less and less need to project ourselves out there, and more and more assurance that through being here, now, we can bring all that we are to bear – in a good way – on the world around us.

So you might like to try this as an exercise. Sit in a quiet room on your own. If you don't have a quiet room, find a pleasant spot to be – on a bridge, or at a gate, or in woods or fields, or on a park bench. Be still, and imagine you were "being there" for someone else. And now, slowly but surely, just imagine "being there" for yourself. Surrender all your preconceptions, opinions, and ideas about who you think you are or should be.

Do nothing more than experience your own presence. Don't overly think about it, don't worry about who or what you are, just be there for yourself, in quiet, gentle appreciation, and sense the person you were created to be, from the very beginning. The person beneath the layers, who doesn't need to try too hard, or prove anything.

Try to enjoy being at home in your own presence. Because once you can do that successfully, no traffic jam, or train delay, or flight cancellation, or time of solitude will ever quite be the same again. It will be an opportunity to reconnect with who you are, and to what matters most to you. In fact, a delay in our schedule is the perfect opportunity to remember that life is not always about getting *there* – so much as being *here*, fully, now, present to all the possibilities that this moment in time can offer.

And present to the possibilities of what you can offer this moment in time in return.

4

Is it true that you want it? Then act like you mean it!

"Being there", as we have noted, is an active thing to do, and it takes great tenacity to continue to be open and present each day to the people we're with and the situations we face. But beyond that, many of us can struggle to act decisively – as if What Matters Most to us really does matter most – because we don't believe that we can close the gap between how we'd love our lives to be and how they really are.

It's crucial, then, to examine the way we see the world, and our place within it, and to remember the extent to which we can hold *ourselves* back from living freely and more fully.

Better-adjusted cogs?

We grow up schooled in a way of thinking and seeing the world. And we can't really help it: our families, friends, teachers, the media, and our institutions all help to shape the way we see life and how we understand our place and role within it all.

Yet it's easy to become so familiar with this way of seeing that we can't see it at all! We settle into a pattern of thinking, and in so doing, we become dulled to the potential we have, within, to act differently. It's tempting to assume that life has always been this way, and that it must continue to be so; that this is just the way things are and forever will be.

And so, when we could be dreaming new and vivid dreams for such a time as this, and bringing our God-given imagination to bear on the issues facing us today, we tend instead to revert to old habits and to set our expectations lower than necessary. "I know what will happen if I try something new," you might protest.

"I'll get it wrong. People won't listen to me. I'll be laughed at. It happened before." (And so on.)

Well, maybe.

Of course, through self-help books and TED talks and the like, we can find very helpful methods of *coping* better with what life has to throw at us. We can discover useful ways of dealing with the complications of life in this fast-changing world; we can try not to become buried by emails, or to burn out, or to be submerged by our to-do list. But since when did we decide to settle for "merely coping"?

The great danger is that we can end up learning simply to become better adapted to survival instead of being who we were put on earth to be and doing what we were put on earth to do, with a flourish and a freedom that is contagious.

Put another way, we can learn how to become better-adjusted cogs – while all the while remaining part of the same old toxic machinery. And surely that's not what we were put on earth to be, is it? Better-adjusted cogs in a machine? There must be more to life than that! A more compelling, free, and creative way to be, part of the problem no more – and demonstrating what it means to be a proactive and creative part of the solution!

Limiting beliefs

One important step toward living more freely and creatively is to become aware of the beliefs we hold about life that are damaging and limiting.

We all have a set of beliefs, whether we like it or not – and these don't have to be religious; we hold beliefs about how the world is organized, where we fit into it, and what difference we can make, for example.

And frequently these beliefs don't focus on pursuing goodness, but instead they create less healthy mindsets; or at best, they can limit our imagination when it comes to what we can do with our lives.

We can hold limiting beliefs together collectively, as a society or a culture (or within organizations or communities), and we can hold them individually. And if we don't become aware of them, they will hold powerful sway over us.

Think about some of the typical limiting beliefs we might have grown up with in Western culture over the last few decades:

"Busy is good, so even if we're not busy, we should look busy."

"You have to be thin to be beautiful."

"We'd all be happier if we had more money."

"To be a leader, you have to be very outgoing and extroverted."

"Spirituality is for tree-huggers and vegetarians."

There are plenty more. Perhaps you can think of some. These are beliefs that can limit the way we see the world, and the way we act within it. And it's easy to tacitly agree with them.

So, limiting beliefs can keep the imagination of an entire culture hemmed in; but they can also be very personal to us, and specific, depending on what we were told and the experiences we had as a child growing up. Perhaps someone suggested to you when you were young that you're not very bright, or even worse, that you were good for nothing. Perhaps you grew up believing that that "girls can't catch" or that "boys don't cry" or...

Here are some limiting beliefs that can affect any of us.

"I don't have what it takes (even though everyone else seems to)."

"I never was any good at... [fill in the blank]"

"I am not creative."

"I am not a 'spiritual' person."

"I never have enough time."

"I will start enjoying life when I retire."

"I was given this job by mistake, and soon they'll find me out."

"It's too late for me to change."

"I don't deserve to be successful."

"Life isn't fair (to me)."

I wonder which of the above particularly resonate with you. And I wonder which other limiting beliefs have held you captive over the years. You might like to spend a few moments reflecting quietly on the things you tell other people or yourself about what you can or cannot do. Write a few down. Or draw a picture to illustrate how such thoughts have limited you. And try, if you can, to become aware of some beliefs you didn't even know you held.

*   *   *

Whenever we act, or react, from our limiting beliefs, we close down the possibilities that life has to offer us. Now, it's easier said than done, of course, but we don't *have* to think automatically in this way. Nothing is stopping us, in theory at least, from pursuing more stretching goals, or to live more adventurous and inspiring lives.

When Roger Bannister famously broke the iconic four-minute-mile barrier in 1954, the scientific world at the time believed it couldn't be done: that the human being had reached the limits of its potential. This is what Bannister observed, some time after the famous race in Oxford, in which he posted a time of three minutes 59.4 seconds:

"Doctors and scientists said that breaking the four-minute mile was impossible, that one would die in the attempt. Thus, when I got up from the track after collapsing at the finish line, I figured I was dead."

He later commented, "There was a mystique, a belief that it couldn't be done, but I think it was more of a psychological barrier than a physical barrier."

Interestingly enough, after Bannister broke through that barrier, another sixteen athletes broke it too in the very same year. Why? Because once the limiting belief had been dismantled, they could train and compete believing it was possible to run a mile in under four minutes.

The sprinter and long jumper Carl Lewis once said, while discussing the seemingly unbreakable record of the long jumper Bob Beamon: "Scientists have proven that it's impossible to long jump thirty feet, but I don't listen to that kind of talk. Thoughts like that have a way of sinking into your feet."

How nimble do you feel right now?

Breaking free

There are certain ways we can try to break free from our limiting beliefs. For instance, you can try this short but effective process:

(a) Write down the limiting belief.

(b) Accept that it's a belief, not a truth.

(c) Apply a different belief to the situation.

(d) *Act as if your new belief is true* (even in taking the smallest step).

You might need to use a journal (or Post-it notes) to remind yourself daily of the limiting belief you are seeking to reframe. And when it comes to applying a "different belief" to your situation, you may need to use your imagination, and to think creatively. Here are a few alternative, empowering beliefs that I have compiled for myself as I have reflected on my own limiting beliefs.

"My work doesn't have to be perfect to be at its most effective."

"It's OK to ask for help. And it's also OK to say no."

"You don't have to be brighter than someone else to be able to help them."

"Most people in my life would like me to flourish."

"Life is not a problem to be solved or fixed."

"I don't have to fight (in the conventional way). The universe is harmonious."

"God is more than I can imagine."

Which of these might help you to live more freely? Which others could you create and record in response to your own limiting beliefs?

* * *

Another approach, after becoming aware of a *limiting* belief, is to find practical examples that contradict it directly. For example, if you're afraid of making presentations because you believe that everything that can go wrong *will* go wrong, ask yourself: How many presentations have I made? What's the worst that happened? How do most of them go? How have people appreciated the way I make them?

One final strategy is to ask yourself how your limiting beliefs have worked against you, and what you might regain by being freed from them. If you grew up believing you weren't creative, for instance, it can be tempting to shy away from creative activity, using the words that people might have spoken about you a long time ago: "Oh, I'm not creative, so…" What has this belief stopped you from doing, and what could you *begin* to do differently if you believed that everyone is creative in their own unique way?

What matters most: that you stay within the comfort zone of what you believe about the world, and don't get found out – or that you open yourself to the possibilities of who you are more fully (even if the results aren't quite as expected)?

Here is one final counter-belief that I came across recently, which has really helped me: "There are no failures, only outcomes – and as long as I learn something, I'm succeeding." This belief helps me to remember that it's important to be open enough to learn from any outcome, whatever happens. A surprising or unexpected outcome can often be far better, in the long term, than one I was *hoping* for or working toward. It requires being open, letting go of my own preconceptions, and remembering to ask: What Matters Most?

* * *

There is great spiritual treasure to be discovered simply through the act of (first) becoming aware of our limiting beliefs and (then) remaining open to the greater possibilities that stretch beyond them.

After all, life is not a problem to be solved or fixed, as we so often think it is – it's so much more. We can't always define or quantify the "more" because we haven't always been able to imagine or experience it. But if we are willing to be open, and to pursue what's **simple, good, and lasting**, and what's waiting for us beyond the confines of our lower expectations, then we have a wonderful chance to break free.

5

Let it go!

We may not know what life really has to offer until we manage to let go of what we believe it *should* offer. And that's not at all easy.

The trouble is, we tend to see the act of "letting go" as an austere, negative process. We are all so used to holding onto things – whether that's to our limiting beliefs, or past triumphs or failures, or simply the physical goods we've accumulated on our journey through life – that to release them seems to go quite against our nature. It actually feels threatening and difficult and sometimes dangerous to do so. Yet if we see letting go as an *art* as much as an act, and if we practise it regularly, we can learn proactively and courageously to *create* more space in our lives for What Matters Most.

*　*　*

Letting go is an ancient spiritual practice, after all, tried and tested by all the great spiritual leaders. Deep down, we can probably sense that much or even most of what we tend to hoard or hold onto for dear life matters less than we like to believe it does. (We spend our lives accumulating things, yet we can't take them with us when we go.)

And while we may not necessarily feel the need to "sell everything … and give the money to the poor" as Jesus once advised a rich young ruler, the gesture or orientation of "release" is nevertheless a powerful way of entering greater personal freedom on a daily basis, to discover more for ourselves of what life beyond our limited expectation holds and more of What Matters Most.

We may not know what life really has to offer until we manage to let go of what we believe it *should* offer. And we may not know what freedom tastes like until we manage to release our grip on what is gripping us.

* * *

The Monkey and the Pebble

Brother Andrew was a Dutchman who became well known later in life for smuggling Bibles behind the Iron Curtain when it was extremely dangerous to do so. He fought, as a young man, for the Dutch resistance during the Second World War in Indonesia, and soon into the fighting, he suffered a bullet wound to his leg. He was nursed by Catholic nuns at a local hospital.

At the time he was deeply disillusioned with his life, depressed, and sullen – but he received some sage counsel in the form of a vivid metaphor from one of his nurses, Sister Patrice, who could see that Andrew had some things to let go of.

"Do you know how the natives catch monkeys out in the jungle?" Sister Patrice began. "No. How?" Andrew replied.

She explained: a monkey won't let go of something once it has grasped it, even if it means losing its freedom. The locals, she said, know this, and are happy to exploit it. They take a coconut and make a hole in it, just big enough for a monkey to slip its hand through, and then they push a pebble through the hole, into the coconut. After that, they place the coconut by a bush and wait for a monkey…

"When a monkey finally comes by," said Sister Patrice, "he is so curious that he picks up the coconut and shakes it. When he hears the pebble inside, he peers in, and then slides his hand through the hole to grasp the pebble. When he tries to pull out his hand still wrapped around the pebble, it will not fit back through the hole. But the monkey will not let go of the pebble, even when the natives approach and capture him."

*   *   *

You might already have a good idea of what, for you, the pebble symbolizes. It might be something that's been said or done to you, many years ago. It might be a false expectation you have held fast to about who or what you should be. It might be what other people think of you. Or a lifestyle you can't afford. Or a regret, or a shattered dream.

We're all clinging to something that keeps us from the freedom that is already ours to experience.

How to let go

But how to let go? Sadly, there is no magic formula, spiritual or otherwise. Instead, perhaps, letting go is a way of being that we can learn, and develop, if we're to get better at it, and if we're to learn not to grasp so tightly and insecurely to what matters less.

Some practical, symbolic gestures *can* be very helpful, however. They won't do the letting go for us, but they will take us closer to the place where we are more willing to loosen our grip.

So, for instance, you could write down what you'd like to let go of on a piece of paper, and then, when you are ready, tear up what you've written, or burn it, or throw it away. Of course, that doesn't mean you've let go of the actual thing itself: but it does help you to acknowledge that you *want* to stop holding on.

Otherwise, here's another way of symbolizing "release". Find yourself a spot by a river, lake, or seafront. (If you can't go there practically, you can always meditatively imagine that you are at a favourite waterside location.) Such places can be helpful and calming in themselves, and just being by water can help to stir the soul and to reconnect us at a deeper level with the world around us.

Find a small stone or pebble, and sit by the water. Hold the pebble tight, like the monkey did. Imagine your pebble to be whatever it is you want to let go of. And then, when you are ready, throw the pebble into the water. Watch it fly, and splash, and disappear. And then choose to leave it there, where you cannot retrieve it.

* * *

Letting go might feel painful, but it is also beautiful

One recent winter, I tried something I've never done before. I leaned against a lovely old tree that still had a handful of leaves left on it, and I looked up, waiting to catch the moment when a leaf is detached from its branch and falls.

There was the slightest breeze, but almost nothing. As I watched, every few minutes or so just one or two leaves would loosen and drop, *so* gently, straight down. This tree was demonstrating how not to cling stubbornly to its once glorious display.

It was a very moving sight, especially as the falling leaf helps to symbolize so vividly our own process of "shedding".

Frequently, we associate the practice of letting go with pain. Either, it feels, we must hand things over reluctantly, like a schoolchild giving in their contraband sweets to a teacher, or we have things ripped from our grasp suddenly, horribly, unexpectedly, in the way a stormy night strips a tree bare in one fell swoop.

But as I stood there in the December stillness of an English field, it struck me, perhaps for the first time, that letting go – even if it's sad – can also be a beautiful, gracious process that we can enter willingly and very naturally.

We suffer most when we try to cling onto things that are passing, whether we like it or not. Happy seasons of our lives that are coming to a close, for instance. Perhaps our children are flying the nest, or our college days are drawing to an end. It's sad. But it's a beautiful thing to let go graciously – and instead of feeling crushed that it's over, we can feel grateful that it happened.

For this to happen, however, we need trust: trust that winter has its place in the process, when the leaves are stripped bare and the landscape widens. Trust that spring will come again. And trust that if we stop clinging to what has come and gone, then we can become more open to the present and to the possibilities and opportunities contained within it.

*   *   *

Letting go can be joyful!

If we practise, we can develop an attitude of joyful generosity that reminds us that nothing is "ours" in the first place, that all must be returned some day, and that we are merely stewards or custodians of what we have for a short time.

Whether it's money, or possessions, or even people. It must be heartbreaking, in a way, for a dad to "give away" his daughter in marriage, because he is losing her. But that process of giving her away reminds us that her presence is a huge gift to her partner, and that a father and mother's loss is a husband or wife's gain.

You might like to give something away. It could, of course, be something you don't need anymore. Such a gift helps you not to become a hoarder. But it might equally be something you *do* still need, but which you know someone else might need more than you. If we can give such a gift generously, joyfully even, then we have entered a new way of being, and are well on the way to discovering and experiencing far more about What Matters Most in the end...

* * *

Stand on a bridge

When I lead retreats, I have found that it really helps to get outside and to seek places or features of the landscape that help us to engage more experientially with the spiritual journey. After all, we're not just taking the journey in our heads.

When it comes to letting go, and to receiving what's still to come with a greater openness, I have found it very helpful to stand on a bridge over a river; preferably, a river that's flowing well.

First, look downstream. Spend some time just being there, with the river; be still, and watch it flow. You might like to practise breathing deeply and slowly, which is a way of helping you to become more present.

You might already know what you need to let go of. Perhaps you are moving jobs, or house, or a delightful season of your life is coming to an end.

The river reminds us that all things must pass, whether they are painful or lovely. Ultimately, we will have to let go of everything. But for now, we must practise letting go of small things and bigger things, as and when we need to. So, keeping in mind what you need to release, watch for a leaf or twig or some flotsam or jetsam, let it symbolize what you need to relinquish, and simply watch it be carried downstream and out of view. Let it go.

And now, go back to staring at the river, letting it speak to you at a deep level about how the river of life takes things away from us. If we can learn to let go without clinging too tightly, we suffer less. The suffering comes from trying to cling to something that must, in fact, be relinquished.

Once you are ready, turn then to face the oncoming stream. This part of the reflection is about welcoming what is to come, with the kind of openness to life that we began to develop in the previous chapters.

Again, watch the river for a few moments, or a few minutes, depending on the time you have. Try not to think too hard about anything.

When you are ready, open your hands and arms a little, to receive symbolically what the river of life is bringing you next. This is a chance to surrender your own plans and schemes, and to open yourself to the possibilities that life itself wants to offer you. Be thankful for what is to come and for what is already right here before you, and ask for wisdom and help to live well within this coming season of your life.

Stepping into the freedom

But what about the freedom that is, in fact, already yours to step into once you *have* let go? What do you think such freedom offers, and what matters more to you: holding onto something that in reality is holding you back in return – or taking your first steps into a world beyond your own self-imposed limits? You may not know exactly what that freedom entails, or where it will take you. That is part of the wonder of letting life come as you also let it go.

6

Waking up to the presence of God

We can be so busy and distracted in life – struggling to stay afloat or to get ahead – that it becomes easy to ignore or forget or neglect the great spiritual energy that pulses like a heartbeat through the universe. Yet if we're considering What Matters Most, why should "God" be left out of the equation?

Imagine, for a moment, you had a tangible Source of energy, inspiration, wisdom, courage, vision, creativity, values, strength… A Source that you could draw from daily, like a well. And imagine, now, that this Source is God. What's stopping you from returning to it, and drawing deeply and profoundly from it, to stay refreshed and renewed for the journey ahead?

Perhaps the problem comes because we have a *mental* image that prevents us from experiencing God in a more positive or vibrant way. It may have to do with the kind of religion you were brought up with, for instance – one that frightened or bored or confused you, perhaps. It might come from the media images that seem to seep into our collective and individual subconscious. The picture of the old man with the long white beard, for instance. Or it might come from the image you have built up of God based firmly on your own experiences of life.

But if life really is best approached with openness and presence, then so, surely, is God. Especially when it's far too easy to assume that we *know* what we mean by God… when perhaps we don't. (At the very least, no one has the full picture, nor the monopoly.)

We all have our own ideas about who God is or isn't, and what God should and shouldn't do, and about why my God might be more ideologically preferable to your God, and all of that.

But preconceptions become lazy, just as entrenched viewpoints become harmful, and any one of us is in danger of suffocating the very possibilities of God. Our beliefs about God become limiting by their very nature, especially when we project these beliefs onto the idea of God.

"God couldn't love someone like *me*..." we might think.

"We don't 'do' God in our family..."

"God wouldn't answer *my* prayer."

But what if God were greater than the sum total of our own insecure projections or cynical preconceptions or deeply entrenched religious claims?

Sometimes, perhaps, we get a glimpse through listening to a piece of music or finding ourselves deep in the heart of nature or experiencing the birth of a child, when the soul stirs and takes us beyond the constricting mental chatter in our heads to a deeper, more poignant place of connection, which is beyond words or explanation, and reminds us of the possibility of the simple, good, and lasting nature of What Matters Most.

A veil is lifted momentarily when for a few moments, seconds, or minutes (these times of clarity rarely last long before we are interrupted), we sense something far beyond us stirring something deep within us.

*   *   *

Who do you imagine God to be?
So, what if there were more to discover about God, and what if that sense of "more" were better than

you could have imagined? What if, as the author and speaker Rob Bell suggests in his book *What We Talk About When We Talk About God*, God is really "with us, for us, ahead of us...", instead of dragging us back or threatening us with imminent punishment or demanding that we dress smartly and behave ourselves?

And what if "finding God" had less to do with discovering religion and more about stumbling upon an astonishing haul of treasure? Imagine, then, how things could change our perceptions.

A Californian couple who were out walking their dog one day in 2014 found a hoard of rare mint-condition gold coins said to be worth more than 10 million US dollars. They didn't walk on by, or frown at their new fortune, or tell themselves it was too good to be true. They dug it up, told the world about it, and delighted in it!

Of course, divine treasure is not to be found in the shape of nineteenth-century golden dollars from the West Coast of the US. Nor will it make us financially rich, or make all our dreams come true. But it's treasure all the same.

When you close your eyes and imagine who or what God is, you probably *don't* picture an old man with a long white beard. But I wonder what any of us expect when we think of, or reach to, or wish for God?

Open to surprise

It's tricky, because when we think of God, our mind works hard to paint a picture made up from everything it has stored that feels relevant. But our minds are subject to the insecure and anxious chattering of the ego, which – when it comes to God – tends to convert God into "our" God, or uses the idea of God to elevate our own identity (God is on our side), or turns God into a genie who exists simply to grant us our wishes.

However, by definition God is beyond what our finite minds are able to comprehend (try even to imagine infinity and we don't get very far), and so we need other ways of experiencing God that, while they don't uncritically reject the work of the mind (which is an instrument of great value when used in the right way), nevertheless enrich and surprise and complement and surpass it.

Sometimes, then, we can only experience more of the possibilities of God by consciously relinquishing the preconceptions that limit our beliefs – and letting go of what we *think* we know about God in order to discover God afresh for ourselves.

In an Easter episode of the much-loved British TV drama *Rev*, about a down-to-earth clergyman struggling to keep a dying inner-city church alive, Revd Adam Smallbone has a stirring encounter with God, who meets him in the form of a homeless man (played by Liam Neeson) in a tatty tracksuit clutching a beer can. It's a beautifully creative and challenging expression of the way we might experience something different about God, even perhaps when we are least expecting it. Perhaps we have already met God, but because it wasn't what we were expecting to see, in a context we didn't think would yield anything "divine", we didn't take a second look.

Becoming centred

It matters, perhaps more than anything, that we become open to who or what God is instead of closed to anything that doesn't fit with our culturally informed ideas. And one of the most helpful practical ways I have experienced of becoming more open to life and open to God is through something called "centring prayer".

All sorts of spiritual methods and practices seem to offer near-magical solutions, which look wonderful on the page until you try them. Please note: centring prayer will not make you successful, good-looking or rich, and it certainly won't solve all your problems. But it will help you to let go, profoundly, of your preconceptions, and prejudices, and limiting beliefs, if you are willing to give it a try: and it will help you to reach for God in greater openness, without agenda.

I recommend this practice whether you are a contemplative Christian, like me, who has his own preconceptions about the nature of God that I need to relinquish, or whether you have no particular affiliation to any creed. Even if you have the faintest willingness to acknowledge the possibility of God, here is an opportunity to be open and curious as to who God is and what God can do…

Open to prayer

First, however, a word about the word "prayer". (We have so many things to unlearn!) It is obviously a word *loaded* with association itself.

You might imagine prayer to be the kind you prayed at school when you were young, when you were told to "put your hands together and close your eyes". You might imagine prayer to be the spiritual equivalent of writing a letter to Santa Claus. Or you might simply imagine that it's a monotonous stream of incomprehensible litanies spoken through a pall of incense at the altar of a cathedral.

But it doesn't have to be. In fact, it doesn't have to be about words at all, which really helps us, once again, to get beyond the incessantly chattering mind to a different place altogether.

Prayer can be many things. Like lighting a candle. Or writing a poem. Or opening your arms. Or staring at the sea. Prayer can be the eating of bread and the drinking of wine, or even the washing of feet.

Let's not reduce prayer to a wishy-washy, lowest common denominator warm fuzzy sensation, however. It's so much more than that, and there is always so much more to discover about a dynamic process that brings us to life. As Brother David Stendl-Raist explains:

"Prayer… is waking up to the Presence of God no matter where I am or what I am doing. When I am fully alert to whatever or whoever is right in front of me; when I am electrically aware of the tremendous gift of being alive; when I am able to give myself wholly to the moment I am in, then I am in prayer. Prayer is happening, and is not necessarily something I am doing. God is happening, and I am lucky enough to know that I am in the Midst." (Quoted in Barbara Brown Taylor, *An Altar in the World*)

Presence. Alertness. The electricity of awareness.

The gift of life. Wholly within the moment. In the Midst. This is the possibility of prayer! And the possibility of prayer opens up the possibility of God to us at a deeper level than our minds can realize.

*   *   *

So, then, to centring prayer. These ideas are based on the inspiring work of the Episcopal priest Cynthia Bourgeault and are expanded upon quite beautifully in her book *Centering Prayer and Inner Awakening*.

Centring prayer is a contemplative form of prayer that's painfully simple, and is based on two things: (1) the intention of being open to God, through (2) the gesture of release.

(This is less about "hands together and eyes closed", and more about sitting in silence for up to about twenty minutes. But as you practise this, you begin to carry the "prayer" around you into everyday life, too.)

Most forms of contemplative prayer (and mindfulness) focus on keeping the mind occupied – through paying attention, whether it's to a short repeated sentence, or to something simple and evocative like a flower or leaf or candle, for example. In paying attention like this, you keep your usually chattering mind busy, and thus you quieten the chatter for long enough to experience a deeper level of consciousness.

Centring prayer, however, is less about holding our attention, and more about focusing our *intention*. And the intention is this: to reach out for God openly.

Nothing more, but nothing less, either.

While this is a simple process, it is nevertheless

profound, and it's a challenge to those of us who like to make things more complex than they ever really need to be.

We reach out to God openly by sitting still and simply "being there" for God and with God, just like we might simply "be there" for a good friend. Just listening. Not trying.

So we sit still, and we sit quietly. And here's the thing: whenever we become conscious that we are thinking about something (which inevitably stops us from being present, because thinking about anything takes us away from where we are mentally), then we let that thought go, and return in openness to God.

We can use a special word, just as in chapter 3 we used a special word to bring us back to being present with other people. You could keep the same word, such as "open" or "present". Or you could choose a word for God or another word that describes this process of being open to God.

Whenever a thought distracts you, speak your special word (out loud or inside), let go of the thought, and return in openness to God.

The good news about this form of prayer is that you don't have to get self-righteous or competitive with yourself about being able to sit there with a thought-free mind. We can't help the thoughts entering our heads and distracting us. But we *can* use them, each time we become aware we're thinking them, to return in openness – meaning that even if you have to "return" sixty times in twenty minutes, every time you do so it's an opportunity to practise openness to God.

And I have found that if you engage this form of prayer regularly, three things happen in particular.

First, you are better able to let go – not only of thoughts, but of anything else that it's helpful to let go of. Centring prayer gently loosens our grip on all the things we might call "mine", such as our plans, our preconceptions, and even our material possessions.

Second, this form of prayer helps us to be more open and curious. It opens up possibilities, expands the imagination, connects us more powerfully with our deeper places.

Third, you may well find that your special word comes to mind when you have become "lost in thought" during the busyness of an ordinary day – when you are having an imaginary conversation with someone about a hypothetical disagreement, perhaps, or when you are raking over the past or fearfully anticipating the future. The word can arrive unbidden to remind us to let go of the unhelpful thoughts, and return in openness...

So why not try it now? Find somewhere to sit quietly, without thinking. When you realize you are thinking, speak your special word, and return in openness to God. And stay with it, for up to twenty minutes.

Hoping for God, from God

What matters most about prayer? Perhaps it's not that we get something out of it, but that we discover something *within* it. And this is where something like centring prayer can really liberate us. It's not about trying to get God to do what we want, or to give us everything on our Christmas list. It's not about the gifts God has to give us at all, in fact (even though it's good and lovely to receive such gifts, with appreciation: imagine what it's like for someone giving their child a present, only for that child to be so fixated about the gift itself that they totally disregard the giver in the process). So instead, this is about discovering and experiencing more about God, full stop. Being there. Just being there, with God.

St Augustine said something very intriguing on this matter, which is summed up very simply in his phrase, "We hope for God, from God."

And that is what we can really do through prayer. Receive God, from God. Sit there quietly, not for gifts, or answers, or direction, or assurance. But for God. And from my own experience, the rest follows, quite naturally.

Detachment from outcomes

If we are truly open to the idea of God, and to reaching out to God, it's good to be detached from the outcomes. In other words, to be willing to be surprised. Because if we are detached from the positive side effects we might crave from prayer or meditation, for example, or to the "answers" or otherwise... then we remain absolutely open to What Matters Most through prayer itself.

7

When things don't go our way

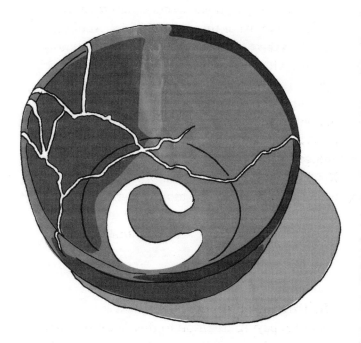

It's so important to go after God, and to go after what's good, and to press in to What Matters Most. But such openness to God, and to life, is not always easy to maintain, especially if you (like most of us) prefer to be in control.

And if you're not sure whether you like to be in control or not, just ask yourself how you feel when your best-laid plans don't work out in the way you want them to.

We all need to plan ahead, of course – it's a necessary and helpful fact of life – whether it's for the short-term, day-to-day stuff, or the broader sweep of where we'd like to end up in terms of career, or family, or the place we live... And some people are better at planning than others. I know of some with a master plan, which takes them right through to early retirement and beyond...

The trouble is, if our master plan becomes "what matters most" to us, there's a great danger we'll feel lost, thwarted, abandoned, or much worse, if and when that plan doesn't work out. (It's funny how often *God* gets the blame when the schemes we have made for ourselves don't come to fruition, isn't it?)

What *are* your plans? And how attached to them are you?

The Unguessed Picture

It's worth paying attention to this, because when we look back at the major events of our lives, it's frequently through the difficult or painful times, and especially those periods during which we have lost control of our future, that we can see how much we have truly grown.

Of course, you can't always tell someone who is being made redundant, for instance, that it will be good for them to lose their job. That's not the point. Instead, our role as a friend in such a situation is to stand with them in their hour of need. But in years to come they may well be in a position to answer with great and unexpected confidence the question: "What did you learn, and how did you grow, through the shock of your redundancy?"

I wouldn't necessarily like to be back in the position in which I found myself a few years ago, when things weren't working out as planned, and I was without a job, or any guaranteed income to speak of. It felt scary and stressful. Yet now, when I look back to that time, not only did I learn a huge amount from losing the usual securities I'd taken for granted – such as how to be more open to life – but I can see now that a richer, more creative plan was unfolding, beyond my own control: a way of working that I could never have dreamed up myself. It's very, very hard to welcome this kind of disruption at the time, of course, but...

The theologian Jaco Hamman speaks of "the unguessed picture" – by which he means a picture we glimpse every now and again, which lies *beyond* the limits of our own imagination and planning. And when we glimpse it, it helps us to make sense of the times when things have not gone according to our own plans.

There is a cost, however, if we're to see more of that picture: we have to relinquish our vice-like grip on what we *think* the future should look like and trust the process instead. For me, as I surrendered my own specific plans, there were practical as well as "spiritual" consequences: a subtly different way of working began to emerge for me, along with a portfolio of projects that I'd never have been able to plan for myself with a sheet of paper and a pen. Very slowly I began to trust both my instinct, and God, and the natural "flow" of the universe, which seemed willing to work with me when I became willing to stop trying to force my own agenda upon it.

This doesn't mean, of course, that we simply abandon ourselves to fate. We must play our part. But the Unguessed Picture reminds us that there is more to life than meets the eye, and we can learn to flow more naturally within it.

Wishing and hoping

Jaco Hamman makes a helpful distinction between wishing and hoping, in fact, which adds some texture here. We know exactly what we wish for, he suggests. Think for yourself, for a moment, about what you find yourself wishing for the most.

I wish... I were somewhere else.

I wish I were better looking.

I wish the weather were nicer.

I wish I had a different job.

I wish I had more money.

I wish we had stayed at home today.

I wish God would...

Wishing is what we end up doing habitually, and for most of the time, whereas **hope** has a very different quality to it. Hope, he says, is "more radically alive to the bigger, Unguessed Picture, the unexpectedly true and beautiful, ever around the corner; to whatever might awaken us to ourselves and each other, undoing our prematurely made-up minds".

When we're hopeful, then, we're willing to acknowledge our limited and egocentric imaginations, and to hope for something greater to emerge beyond them. And that's when it gets really, really interesting.

*   *   *

Think back to a time, then, when you were not in control of your own destiny, when your plans had not worked out. How did you feel at the time? What have you learned, and how have you grown, when things haven't gone all your own way? What good and unexpected things emerged as a result?

And bearing this in mind: how can you learn not to panic, the next time plans go awry; and – even within the moment itself – to welcome instead the growth that will accompany such unsettling times of change, as well as hopeful glimpses of the Unguessed Picture?

The Golden Seam

It's hard not to see beyond the short-term effects of our plans not working out – financial insecurity, a loss of face, grief, illness, whatever it is. And we are likely to bear the scars of what we have been through. But sometimes it is precisely through our brokenness or failing or things not working out that the greatest beauty is most powerfully revealed through our lives.

The Japanese have an ancient craft called *kintsugi*, which is about repairing damage to broken china. Kintsugi craftsmen don't throw out a bowl or a teapot when it is broken. They repair it: but not in the way we might think.

They don't put it back together in order to hide the damage. Instead, they repair the china with a lacquer that is laced with powdered gold, so that the cracks and the joins become visible seams of gold. When the object has been pieced back together, then, the brokenness is acknowledged and honoured – and this process, and this acceptance, creates something *even more beautiful* than it ever was in the first place.

We are all, in our own way, broken. We bear the scars, especially when the best-laid plans so often go astray. But it's through these times that we frequently begin to discover more, for ourselves, of What Matters Most.

* * *

Start from here

If we allow ourselves to get frustrated, anxious, or angry about life not going according to plan, we run the great risk of not accepting (on an ongoing basis) the parts of our lives that don't fit with what we believe our lives should look like... And for those of us with a faith, the accompanying pitfall is that we're forever tempted to create a religion from the most positive aspects of our lives, while trying to ignore or deny or suppress the most "negative". (Many people think that if life doesn't go to plan, then they must have done something bad to deserve it.)

We'll never be transformed, and neither will our situation, however, if we simply keep masking the reality of life. (That's why the first step for recovering alcoholics is to acknowledge they are alcoholic. They cannot move beyond their situation until they become present to it.) Denial creates for us (at best) a double life, which often becomes a far more tangled and complex web of deceit... in which we're kidding not just others but ourselves that things are better than or different to how they really are. And that's because we're still caught up with picturing how we think our lives *should* be.

As Brené Brown suggests in her powerful book *The Gifts of Imperfection*, "When we spend a lifetime trying to distance ourselves from the parts of our lives that don't fit with who we think we're supposed to be, we stand outside of our story, and hustle for our worthiness by constantly performing, perfecting, pleasing and proving."

Wishing we were someone else, or some place else, will never allow us to start from where we are – which is the only place we truly can start from if we wish to move on. And there's a form of prayer that can help us to be present to whatever situation we face, especially when it's not the one we expected.

Welcoming prayer

Centring prayer has a cousin called "welcoming prayer", which helps us to embrace the reality of how we're feeling in any given situation, as the moment itself arises. (Again, you can practise the principles of this discipline, whether you have religious belief or not.) It helps us to respond from a place of deeper assurance, instead of from the usual insecure turbulence of our egocentric mind. This doesn't, by the way, mean we must actively welcome, for instance, the diagnosis of an illness, but the *emotions* that arise from such news.

And this can make all the difference between spiritual escapism – constantly wishing things were different – and *transformation*, which emerges so often from deep within the difficulties of everyday life.

Step one is to focus in immediately on how the feeling is affecting you, and in particular your body. Do this as soon as your emotions have been aroused. Is your jaw clenched? Do you have a knot in your stomach? Is your blood pumping? Don't try to change anything; just be present to this physical sensation, aware of it, focused upon it.

Step two is to "welcome" the emotion, from a position of what Cynthia Bourgeault calls "inner hospitality" or assurance. "By embracing the thing you once defended yourself or ran from, you are removing its power to hurt you or chase you back into your smaller self," she says. You can do this by simply repeating over, "I welcome you, fear." Or, "I welcome you, anger."

"I welcome you…"

Third, you gently let it go. You can say quite simply, "I let go of my anger." Or, if you prefer, "I give my anger to God." You might also say, "I let go of my desire to change the situation." Which helps you, in that moment, to relinquish the need for this to be a fix-it prayer, and instead to remain fully present to God, and to the Unguessed Picture, within the immediate turmoil. So:

> focus in;
>
> welcome;
>
> let go, or give to God.

The welcoming prayer helps us to face turbulent situations in a more assured way, from a more centred place within. And at the same time, it weaves in a beautifully practical pattern of being present *within* our daily routine.

It's good to have goals – but savour the steps to completing them

Sometimes when I go out for a run, I find myself wishing it's over before it has begun, so I can get back to my desk – despite the fact that this time, for me, is when I experience the most creative, insightful, and spiritually significant passage of the day.

We can wish so many things finished before they've hardly begun, can't we? Like the bus or train ride you might be on right now. Or the rest of a difficult week. (You might even catch yourself rushing through these words, knowing you've more urgent things awaiting your attention.)

The point of this journey is *not* to get through it, but to break up our busyness-as-usual routine, and to discover more of What Matters Most within it.

We have talked in this chapter about what happens when we cling too hard to our plans. That doesn't mean it's not helpful and important to have great goals – which are like plans, but with even sharper focus. I coach people to help them establish goals that are "smart" – specific, measurable, achievable, realistic, and time-specific. The one danger with knowing where you wish to get to, however, is to spend all your time wishing you were there already, instead of being present to every step involved in getting there.

In running itself, goals help to sharpen your training, and keep you motivated. They provide focus to your regular exercise, and you can measure how well you are doing. But unless you try to savour the process of being out there, in the sun and the rain, whatever the weather, then the goal is almost worthless. For what does it matter, really, whether you break a certain time barrier? It's the way we try to get there that helps to define the very nature of our journey through life.

8

Spend the afternoon – counter-intuitive ways of being

Sometimes it helps to do something positively and specifically countercultural in order to remind us that the process of getting there is what helps to define the nature of our journey.

"Do not be afraid to waste time with God," said the dusty pamphlet I found one day at an empty wayside church. (It's funny how the seemingly insignificant little things can speak profoundly.) And wasting time is certainly countercultural enough!

Time – and especially its passing – can tyrannize us, whether it's a stressful schedule, tight deadlines, or just the dread of growing older. But that pamphlet reminded me of a line from the contemplative writer Annie Dillard, who once said, quite simply: "Spend the afternoon. You can't take it with you." She surely didn't mean "pack it full" – but savour it, luxuriate in it. Be within it. Watch it.

And if we're not *too* stretched to notice, a strange thing seems to happen when we do. In our busy world, although it may feel such a waste to be still, or to enter silence, or to go for a walk and pray... we can find ourselves with more time on our hands than we realized we had: for we become less rushed, more present; less reactive, more proactive; less "busy", more focused.

Annie Dillard happens to live next to a creek, and her simple aim, as a contemplative, is "to look well at it", and thus to become more fully present to it. That's What Matters Most to her. Not to win literary prizes, or to make a name for herself (though she's done both!); but to "look well" at the place where she lives, and so, to show up; to be here, now.

Perhaps such a countercultural goal could help to inspire you to reflect on the nature of your own goals in life, and whether they need rethinking.

* * *

When she's living in the present, Annie Dillard says she is open to receive more of what the place, the world, life itself, has to give. But there's a way of doing this that speaks powerfully of *how* we could pursue the matter of What Matters Most.

"You don't run down the present," she writes, from huge experience. "[You don't] pursue it with baited hooks and nets. You wait for it, empty handed, and you are *filled*..." She concludes: "You'll have fish left over."

Many of us complain of having our hands full. For me, that means having a full schedule, too much on. "I have my hands full," I'm prone to saying, "so I'm afraid I can't..." And when things are full, my default is to have things planned out. Which means there is often little room to expect the unexpected, or – more importantly – to receive the unexpected with open hands of welcome when it arrives.

Believe in miracles (and live as if you do!)
The activist Shane Claiborne, whom we mentioned earlier, not only imagines how the world *could* look different; he contrives to bring that world alive, within him, and around him. We looked at a few of his simple but challenging "resolutions" previously. But here's perhaps both the hardest *and* the most creative:

"Believe in miracles," he writes, "and live in a way that might necessitate one."

It's easier to do the first bit of this than the second. Anyone can believe in miracles. But to live in a way that might necessitate one? That speaks, to me, of living in such a way that you can't help but begin to see the Unguessed Picture emerge.

Not that we should seek miracles for the sake of it – they prove little, aside from our temptation to put God to the test, as Jesus was tempted to in the desert. Miracles are not about getting God to perform magic on demand, and we should beware trying.

Nevertheless, it's fair to say that the way we live reflects the level of trust we invest in God, and in each other, and in the universe. Shane's resolution reminds me that I often seek security before anything else – trying not to rely too much on anyone, just in case.

I've little experience of miracles, but they tend to happen most when we relinquish control, don't they? And they seem to be less about the flash of a wand, and more about the grace of others. I was helped, miraculously, by a man near Belfast once; but it was only when I could no longer help myself – stranded without a phone down a country road (long story), desperate and without a clue how to get home to my wife and newborn daughter in England when the planes were grounded by volcanic ash. That was the point I became faintly receptive to a miracle (not that I'd dared to hope).

The spit-and-sawdust man, who hailed from the wrong end of the city, passed me in the car, did a U-turn, and invited me to get in. I obeyed, in trepidation. The miracle was, I accepted! I put myself in his care.

This man calmly listened to my story, and formed a plan for me. He took me to the ports, got me booked onto the next day's boat, and then helped me to find a hotel for the night. When I asked him, finally, why he'd stopped in the first place, he said, "Because I thought God told me to." So it turns out he was taking the biggest risk of the two of us.

Perhaps the miracle itself is to live in a way that might necessitate one. After that, maybe, anything can happen.

9

Beyond words

Once we are open to the possibility that What Matters Most lies beyond our limited imagination and egocentric ideas about life, there are practical ways we can look more helpfully for a Wisdom that is so much more than words; to connect with a deeper Source that confounds the usual categories of rational human thought...

*   *   *

Obfuscate. It's a great word, obfuscate. And we do it a lot. It means "to make obscure, unclear, or unintelligible". Or "to bewilder". And we're well practised at it. Either because we're so desperate to fill any silence or void with chatter and noise that we say too much, *or* because we try to make life more complex than it needs to be, for fear that we'll look stupid. But the very words we use often keep us locked in a conceptual prison, instead of releasing us into the realm of experience, and thus toward transformation.

Perhaps words are like the sherpa-led mules that carry a climber and their equipment into the foothills of a great mountain range. They can take you so far, but no further. If we want to continue our ascent, there is a point at which we must leave behind the safety and companionship of those words and sentences, of the books and essays, of the endless talks and lectures, to find a different way of knowing, and sensing, and reconnecting with What Matters Most, for ourselves.

And that quest, in the end, must draw us into the practice of silence. For within silence, we discover a presence that words cannot describe. It's unexplored territory for many of us: a different realm, which – the longer we inhabit it – becomes less about the absence of noise, and more about the *presence* of something beyond the noise.

Centring prayer, which we introduced earlier, is one very simple way to enter silence meaningfully. It helps us to deal with the incessant thoughts that fill our mind and gatecrash the silence – and which so often deter us from being still for long. You can use the simple technique of Centring Prayer – letting thoughts go, to return in openness to God and to life – alongside any opportunity to enter silence and stillness (and we'll consider one or two examples now). It will help you to notice just how often your egocentric mind tries to fill the space with chatter, and to practise moving beyond words into a place of richer connection with the Source of your life.

Ways to enter silence

So let's not obfuscate: there are some simple ways of entering silence, which need not be in any way religious, but can helpfully strip away the various layers that get in the way.

If you're not used to spending time in silence, try starting with smaller chunks of time. After all, we're not competing to see who can maintain silence for the longest, or who is the most spiritual in the class. You could build a few moments' pause – perhaps three longer breaths in and three longer breaths out – before each meal, for instance, in order to help you to become more present to the blessing of food and to the smells and tastes of what you are about to eat. That pause can be a "thank you" as well as a moment to reconnect and to be more present; and it can help you to establish very quickly and easily a gentle rhythm that incorporates silence.

Instead of putting music on during a walk, you could instead engage your senses proactively along the way, one at a time. To start with, try noticing what you can hear. Give thanks for it. A little while later, see what you can see (and what you might have missed if you weren't practising being "present"). Then, ask yourself what you can smell. The olfactory sense is so visceral: the smell of freshly cut grass, or the first salty whiff of sea air, or the wafting fragrance of bluebells on a warm woodland evening in May... smell is *so* connective. Then, finally, notice what you can feel. The breeze on your face or arms; or how your legs might be aching, or how your blood is pumping. This will help you to be *here* – not swept away on a torrent of mental chatter, but powerfully present. Notice what it feels like to be *alive*.

Silence in groups (sensing the presence, not the absence)

It's profoundly important to cultivate the time you spend alone in silence (especially if you are an extrovert who rarely gives yourself the time or space to do so). But observing silence as a group can be equally inspiring if you are willing to try it.

Recently, I led a silent retreat that spanned three days. At first, the lack of talking felt awkward. Most of us were self-conscious. After all, it's unusual for a group of ten or so people to be together and not to share the usual pleasantries that fill those in-between moments, or to discuss the weighty spiritual matters we might otherwise have done. This was especially noticeable at meal times, when you'd normally expect the chatter to drown the chinking of cutlery.

But it's fascinating, and eye-opening, to watch the group dynamics work differently in such a context. You'd expect the talkers to dominate the conversation, and the jokers to make wisecracks, and the introverts to blend slowly into the wallpaper (as I like to do), and so on. But not this time. Silence strips us of the roles we revert to; and so we began to discover a different way of being together.

Each meal became more graceful, like a dance, with the group thinking and moving more and more effortlessly, almost as one, without speaking: sensing, connecting, pre-empting, passing what was needed without needing to be asked, clearing away, and all the while "being" with each other in a gentler, more intimate way. We were intuiting, empathizing, reading each other, and managing to be there together at a soulful, instead of purely conversational, level as a group.

You could easily try this. Spend time in silence as a family or a friendship group or small group. Practically, you might need to acknowledge there'll be tummy rumbles or unexpected noises occasionally... And remember that it's OK to smile and laugh, too; silence doesn't have to mean you lose your sense of humour and become as one-dimensional as a cardboard cut-out.

The first time I encountered group silence in a larger context was when the Franciscan priest Fr Richard Rohr spoke at Westminster Cathedral in London. He was addressing several hundred people on the theme of "Silence in the City" – exploring how to embrace silence within the noise and hustle of city life. And after his short talk, he guided us into a whole twenty minutes' worth of silence. This was an astonishing experience, and one that has inspired me, since, to lead all sorts of larger groups, whether in churches, or even (and especially) corporate workshops and events, into "plenary" silence. It takes a little courage at first, as most of us believe that sitting, doing nothing, is a complete waste of time; that we should be doing *something*. And it usually takes the first few minutes of stillness for most people to get used to just being there, quietly. But as they do, a different kind of space seems to open up, qualitatively... in which you sense a palpable presence, instead of an absence.

Manual work

Another way to pursue What Matters Most beyond the realm of words and ideas and the usual concepts is through manual labour.

Or so argued the author Tobias Jones when I interviewed him about a book he'd written called *Utopian Dreams*. He'd spent a year living in different (intentional) spiritual communities around the world. And he told me that by far the most effective communities were those that included manual work as part of the daily rhythm of community life.

Whether that meant chopping firewood, planting hedges, building stone walls... he noticed that the work had both a cathartic and galvanizing effect on people individually and as a whole. (Let's not forget that such manual work is considered a vital part of the daily spiritual rhythm of most monastic orders.)

When I suggested to him that it was unrealistic, in our wired-in consumerist world, to expect people to engage ordinarily in regular manual work as a spiritual practice, he challenged me. Why not? We may be increasingly disconnected from the work of our hands (aside from typing) – but aren't we also feeling displaced, fretful, anxious, restless...? It's not easy to sleep after a day sat staring at screens. We slip from computer work to twiddling with smartphones, to channel-surfing TV and fiddling with tablets, and then we wonder why we don't feel at peace. But after a day outside digging, or tearing down, or building up, it's a different matter altogether.

It's not primarily about getting jobs done. There is a strong resonance between rhythmic labour and meditation, and repetitive physical work can help to carry the centredness of meditation into daily life.

I have been on spiritual retreat with others as we have helped to fell trees and shift dead wood. That *was* our work, our offering, our prayer, our way of being for a day; it pulled us together, it tired us out, and it got us out of our egocentricity and into a flow we'd otherwise not have found in mere discussions or conversations.

Would that it were more complex, more clever, more sophisticated! But sometimes we can't see What Matters Most for looking, because it's formed within the wordless world... in this case, of muscle and sweat, fetching and carrying, serving and supporting, friendship and toil.

And it reminds me, each time I'm tempted to shirk a physical task such as digging over the raspberry patch to embrace it instead, and to offer the very physicality of the work – no more! – as a prayer, or meditation, and to find within it the clarity, simplicity, and sense of fulfilment that so often eludes us as we stare blearily into our screens. After all, what's the point in talking or writing about life unless we can get our hands dirty every now and again?

Pay attention to what we feel through the body

The body is too often dismissed when it comes to "spirituality" – at best it's seen as a mere vehicle for spirit, and at worse, a constant source of impure desire that gets in the way of "pure" spirituality, and which must be battled and overcome. Yet we live in a physical world, within a Creation that God (according to the Bible, at least) declared to be "good". And when we stop to think of it, some of the most palpable and visceral ways of discovering What Matters Most surely do arrive through the body, whether that's through agony, or ecstasy, or somewhere in between.

Deep suffering, says the priest and author Barbara Brown Taylor, makes theologians of us all. To spend one night in serious pain is to discover depths of reality that are out of reach while everything is fine. So we ask, "Why me? Why now? Why this?"

It's natural for us to do so, she says. However: such questions should be just as relevant when we are in pleasure. "Who deserves the way a warm bath feels on a cold night after a hard day's work?" she asks. "Who has earned the smell of a loved one, embracing you on your first night home?"

I've found that physical exercise such as running – just as with manual work – can be a profound a way of helping me to slow down my mind, become more present, and renew my emotional and spiritual energy while spending physical energy. And I've noticed that time and again, the most significant creative breakthroughs come, for me, not when I'm sat at a computer screen, but when I'm exerting myself physically.

Many people report the same thing. Physical exercise gives you a break from the compulsive thinking that accompanies so much of the short-term, quick-fix mental work we attend to in life, as well as a break from the interruptions that arrive through our phones and computers. It therefore allows us to enter a deeper level of consciousness, below the busy surface, and to access the more creative areas of our conscious and subconscious self. When I'm running, I don't try to think things though – I have learned that the best ideas are the ones that simply arrive without thinking too hard about them, from seemingly out of nowhere.

The physical body, then, plays as much a part in the process of deeper creative connection as the mind. This is crucial to understand and acknowledge. It's not an esoteric or exclusively intellectual process, thank God, this business of travelling toward the heart of What Matters Most. Our physicality is, in so many ways, our spirituality and – to speak personally – my daily run has become one of a handful of things that matter most for me in life – *because* of that sense of deeper connection it brings, and the creative insight that accompanies it. That's not to say that everyone should be a runner, of course – you will find your own way of searching for What Matters Most. But it will include a physical search if it is to be fully whole.

"Sometimes," suggests Barbara Brown Taylor, "*we do not know what we know* [my italics] until it comes to us through the soles of our feet, a tender embrace or the kindness of a stranger."

The language of nature

What is it about nature that helps to ease our passage toward What Matters Most? If we're feeling stressed or uptight or distracted, we know, deep down and intuitively, that it will do us good to get outside in the fresh air and spend a few minutes standing on a beach or walking through a field or sitting against a tree. Somehow it resets and restores us; we gain perspective.

And that's not just because the scenery might be lovely or soothing or inspiring, although of course it's great when it is. Instead, it's because nature speaks to us in the richest language, without and beyond words. The power of a storm. The stillness of a snow fall. The majesty of a sunset. The spectrum of a rainbow. It all whispers to us at a soulful level, in a way that we might not even consciously understand.

But that's OK. In fact, it could be a blessing. Even if we wanted to appear smart before nature, we can't. Try to stand before a tree and impress it with how cool you are. Try to bend it with a clever argument. Trees simply are, as waves simply are, as animals simply are, as the clouds simply are... And in their simply being, they draw us to a place deeper within us, further toward our hidden Source. When we find ourselves here, we simply are, too.

Stop looking for the answers

Do not expect to find all the answers of this world, 'cos if we could somehow, and then we did, who would we be anyway?

(Martyn Joseph, "Let Yourself")

The singer-songwriter Martyn Joseph recorded a gorgeously soulful song called "Let Yourself" (which we will return to in our final chapter). It contains this profound line, above, which has truly liberating consequences – if we are to believe it.

Usually, if we go on a retreat, or find ourselves searching proactively for a deeper spiritual connection between our own life and the "unguessed picture", then we'd think it was perfectly reasonable that our search should involve looking for an answer. In fact, I have led plenty of retreats myself in which people have come looking for an answer but have not received it as directly as they would have liked.

There's nothing wrong in itself with hoping for a specific answer to your questions or to your prayers. It's just that it doesn't always arrive like that. We have come to expect that it should – because in the context of our rational, post-Enlightenment world, we've been programmed to believe that when a question forms, there's a right answer to be discovered. But this supposes that life is a problem to be solved. And we can end up thinking that if *only* we could answer more of life's questions, we'd start to work this life out much better. Yet don't those who are wiser often say that the older they get, the less they know...?

Imagine you *did* have all the right answers. What would you do with them? And who would you be? Do the answers matter most? And if not, then what...?

Let your soul sing

We simply can't wait until we have all the right answers before we start living fully – for it's the process of making the journey itself that reveals more to us of the truth of What Matters Most along the way. So we can be released from thinking that we have to search for a right answer (which is what paralyses so many of us – what happens if we can't find it, or get it wrong, or take a wrong turn, or miss the point altogether?). The search, instead, becomes the answer: a unique creative expression of our exploration.

It's in the searching, it's in the doing, it's in the responding, that we discover more of who we are, and of What Matters Most to us. That's why creativity is important along the way: it helps us to express something uniquely of our soul, even as we go in search of what our soul is like. *We find our soul when we let our soul begin to sing.*

In fact, I have frequently observed that when people take time out to reflect on their spiritual journey or to "retreat", they don't come away clutching the answers; instead, they experience an unblocking of their creativity. Something starts to flow within them once more. They start to paint or sketch or write poetry or sculpt or sew or do gardening or make music or take photographs. Spiritual awakening seems to go hand in hand with creativity: as we awaken, we start to create; and as we start to create, we awaken. It's through expressing something creatively that we can see it for ourselves, often as if for the first time.

Sadly, in the West our creativity has been stifled, especially in a culture in which we see ourselves as consumers first and foremost. Coupled with this is a reluctance many of us have to express anything much of ourselves soulfully or artistically, for fear of what other people might think; for fear that it's not "good" enough, or that we might give too much of ourselves away.

And so, many of us have slowly closed up. Yet within each of us lies the creative potential to respond to life by opening once more, and to inspire others to do likewise.

*   *   *

Spirituality is not just about painting pictures, of course, or making great art. Our creative response to the spiritual search helps to shape the imaginative and creative nature of our actions, too. Remember: we do not wish simply to become better-adapted cogs, but to become radically part of the solution in this life.

"There is a vitality, a life force, a quickening," writes the choreographer Martha Graham, "that is translated through you into action, and because there is only one of you in all time, this expression is unique. If you block it, it will never exist through any other medium and be lost. The world will not have it. It is not your business to determine how good it is; nor how valuable it is; nor how it compares with other expressions. It is your business to keep it yours, clearly and directly, to keep the channel open."

As we free up our creativity, then, the very search for What Matters Most itself, which may have begun as a question, imperceptibly shifts to *embody* that which we can offer back to the world around us through our own creative, compassionate life.

We show the world What Matters Most to us by acting as if we mean it.

10

Walking the talk: embodying the spiritual journey

Most journeys today are about getting us from A to B as expediently as possible. The spiritual journey, however, is not like this, and we should beware treating it as such; as if it were like an aircraft ride, perhaps, to a different continent, during which we can read a novel and watch a movie, before disembarking to enjoy the sights.

The spiritual journey instead takes a different form altogether, drawing us deeper, not always sending us further; slowing us down, instead of accelerating our passage. It means learning to be *here*, rather than constantly straining to get "there".

The lost art of sauntering

The way we walk – literally – can help us to begin to embody the very different nature of this journey, and reveal more about it to us. Pilgrimage is an ancient tradition in all the major religions for good reason: there is nothing like a long slow walk for reconnecting, somehow, with What Matters Most; with regaining a sense of perspective, and seeing the world first hand, without it whizzing by in a blur through a car window, or in a flurry of TV images.

We don't have to make pilgrimage to a far-off land, however, to slow down the pace and experience something very special indeed. A *saunter* can open our eyes very beautifully to the fact that wherever we find ourselves, we can begin to see the world around us vividly through fresh eyes.

The word saunter comes from the French phrase "*a la sainte terre*" – meaning to the holy land or ground, according to Henry David Thoreau. Pilgrims in

medieval times became known as "Sainte Terrers"...
who became, over time, "saunterers".

As such, then, a simple saunter today can capture
the essence of pilgrimage – which is not all about
arriving somewhere, but *making the journey* –
mindfully, prayerfully, purposefully – and all the while
embodying the nature of our journey through life
itself. As we'll see through the exercise below, when
we physically start to walk mindfully, prayerfully,
purposefully, it becomes quite quickly apparent that
our "destination" was not so far away at all: in fact,
the very ground we stand upon is sacred, if we could
but realize it. But this isn't something we can simply
know in our head; we only discover the treasure of
sauntering by trying it ourselves.

A slow walk of awareness

So try taking a slow walk.

A short, slow walk. You can do this in a country
setting (it's always lovely to saunter through a
meadow, for instance, and to notice how many
different insects or grasses you can see, or the
variety of birds you can hear), but it can be *especially*
powerful to walk slowly within a busy town or city
centre.

The idea is to walk along a short stretch that you
might normally associate with getting from A to B.
Somewhere you might otherwise march through
unthinkingly, without pausing, as you get on with
your day. Identify a length of road or pavement
that would take you perhaps two or three minutes
to speed past.

And then start walking – but take at least twice as long as normal to get to "B", slowing yourself right down, and allowing yourself to become aware, as you go, of what you are noticing, as if for the first time.

You're likely to feel self-conscious at first, and to focus on what people think of you. Do I look silly? What if I meet someone I know? What will they think of me? That's the overprotective voice of your egocentric mind, worrying on your behalf. (It's hard not to feel like you stand out, when you slow down, as everyone else seems in such a rush to get somewhere.) You might also notice how hard it is simply to slow down, and how tempting it is to speed up again!

But stay with it, for gradually you're likely to start noticing details you've never seen before, hidden within all that's familiar: tiny details on the pavement, in doorways or windows, up at roof level, even. You notice conversations. And smells. And you start to settle into the slower pace. *It's not that bad, after all.* And then, finally, perhaps you begin to notice the usually unnoticed details on people's faces, too. They're not masks anymore, floating past – but people. "Behind every face, there is something eternal going on," writes the philosopher and poet John O'Donohue, and if you look, you will now begin to see this for yourself. And if you are present to what's happening inside you, as well as outside, then you may also start to feel renewed compassion welling up for this world you've rarely stopped to notice, these brothers and sisters of yours – and you may also experience a sense of love arising that you hardly realized you were capable of.

All this from taking a slower walk than usual.

We can be so preoccupied with trying to get somewhere in life as fast as possible that we miss the fact that, as St Catherine of Siena is reputed to have said, "The path to heaven lies through heaven, and all the way to heaven is heaven."

Every step counts, in other words. Remember, *this* journey is not from A to B. It is an embodiment of the spiritual movement we make toward What Matters Most, and it *could* help to change the feel of your day, your week, your year, or even your life.

X marks the spot

Much of our dissatisfaction in life, and much of our stress, and much of the rush, comes from the misplaced idea that if we only had more, or if we only had what other people have, or if only we were someone else or somewhere different, then we'd be OK. Life would somehow make sense. So we spend our energy chasing after what we don't have, as if *that's* What Matters Most: what we *don't* have.

Yet here's the spiritual twist, the treasure that's waiting to be discovered within the ordinary, everyday, familiar context that we find ourselves: when we cease trying to get more of what we don't really need, it frees up our energy to make a difference with what we already have. And that difference can grow and grow.

It's a challenge to love what we already have, because the messages in our consumer culture teach us that everything goes out of date quickly and needs updating and replacing. I upgraded my smartphone recently, which gave me a temporary thrill – but quickly I caught myself thinking forward to when the *next* upgrade would be, and realizing that I was, in a way, already disregarding what I'd only just purchased. The consumer mindset feeds on dissatisfaction – with what we own, what we look like, and more perniciously still, who we are.

The US pastor Barbara Brown Taylor puts it like this. "No one longs for what he or she already has," she writes. "And yet the accumulated insight of those wise about the spiritual life suggests that the reason so many of us cannot see the red X that marks the spot is because we are standing on it."

"The treasure we seek," she concludes, "requires no lengthy expedition, no expensive equipment, no superior aptitude or special company. All we lack is the willingness to imagine that we already have everything we need. The only thing missing is our consent to be where we are."

So while we are setting out positively and proactively to look for What Matters Most, it couldn't matter less, in a sense, where we get to. The destination is not some longed-for heavenly hideaway, some kind of gated community where our problems disappear and we can sit dreamily without a care, protected from what's difficult or (heaven forbid) ordinary; What Matters Most is *here*. And it's *now*.

* * *

Here and now
Our ordinary, everyday life matters, then – because it's where we spend most of our time, and it's what we can

waste most of our energy wishing away. It is our very "here" and "now".

And so the way we *see* our everyday life is critical because – almost unthinkingly – if we believe "ordinary" is dull or second best, then we end up selecting our most memorable, outstanding, and successful moments in life in order to create a story that feels more significant than it ever needs to be. It's like putting together the TV highlights "package" at the end of a sports event such as the Olympics.

Yet compiling a narrative of our highlights means we're still a long way off savouring what is here and now, because with such a mentality, we are unconsciously looking "over there" – into the future – for the next moment to add to the package; living for the weekend, when we're going out, or for the summer, when we're off on our holidays. Living for the next purchase, or the next "moment" we can stick up on Facebook as a change in status.

Imagine, however, that What Matters Most were not to be found in the story of the best bits at all, but hidden like treasure, all along, in the way we spend most of our lives, within the everyday tasks, within the rhythms of the days, the weeks, the months, the seasons, within the seemingly insignificant interactions with other seemingly insignificant people, within the beautiful ordinariness of it all.

How would it change the way you were to see your morning, your afternoon, or your evening, if you knew that there were treasure hidden within it, waiting to be discovered by seeking it in this, your here and now? What story could you tell about your ordinary life that was somehow more powerful, authentic, and "you" than simply the story of the best bits?

Bumping into God

"We all have moments when we glimpse something beyond the purely material world, when we 'bump into God'" writes the down-to-earth vicar and author Dave Tomlinson. "But we don't necessarily think of them as religious or spiritual experiences." On the spiritual journey, in other words, we might still be tempted to look "over there" for God – but we don't have to.

We can bump into God in the ordinary "sacred" moments – which can be joyful, sad, inspirational, melancholic, awesome. Here is a list he compiled. You might like to take each line slowly, as you read it, and try to imagine you are there:

> "receiving an undeserved smile from a child;
> gazing at the Milky Way on a dark night far from city lights;
> holding the hand of a dying loved one;
> gazing at a city cleansed by a recent fall of snow;
> weeping over a broken relationship;
> sipping a cold beer on a summer day, with nothing to do;
> feeling inspired by a new project;
> hearing a blackbird sing as dusk falls in winter;
> standing at an open grave."

What could you add?

Dave delivers a great challenge. "How can we aspire to some holy life if we can't find God in simple things like a glass of beer, a warm bath, a good kiss, a belly laugh, a hug with a friend...?"

How indeed? In other words, the most ordinary stuff of life can point – like bread, wine, or water – mysteriously and powerfully to God. But God, in return, points mysteriously and powerfully back to the most ordinary stuff of life. To what might matter most, in the end.

* * *

Martyn Joseph's beautiful song "Let Yourself" has a lovely refrain, which draws from the poet Rumi: "Let yourself be quietly drawn by the stronger call of what you really love," he sings. Not by the pull of the ego toward what everyone else thinks should matter most; nor by the fears that push us into a corner, and hem us in, and exhort us to cling for dear life to all the things that really won't matter much at all in the end. But let yourself be quietly drawn by the stronger call of *what you really love*.

It may not be immediately obvious – it can be hard to discern what we really love, because we may feel it's all too simple, or perhaps it's almost too obvious to see. At other times we are distracted or searching too hard for a right answer instead of entering a joyful flow of presence in which we can explore and express more of who we've been created to be. But ultimately it is love that will help us to discern, more than anything, What Matters Most.

124

What we love reveals what God loves about us

In her life-affirming book *One Thousand Gifts*, Ann
Voskamp, who suffered tragedy early in her life and
who struggled honestly to accept the reality of life –
and God – being "good", dared herself:

"Could I write a list of a thousand things I love? To
name one thousand blessings – one thousand gifts."
So she took a piece of paper and started writing, "on a
whim, a dare. I begin the list. Not of gifts I want but of
gifts I *already have*.

> "1. *Morning shadows across the old floors.*
> 2. *Jam piled high on toast.*
> 3. *Cry of blue jay from high in the spruce.*

*"That is the beginning," she continues, "and I smile. I
can't believe how much I smile. I mean, they are just the
common things... This writing down – it is sort of like...
unwrapping love. It might fit like a glove."*

What a picture! And this is a beautiful observation.
That the goodness and love that surrounds us is so
wrapped up in the ordinary and so fully envelops us
that we may struggle to see it unless we specifically
start to express it for ourselves.

I started writing a list myself.

1. Playing football with my son and daughter.

2. Climbing trees with my kids.

3. Sitting by the beach, staring out to sea.

4. The feel of lush grass as I walk barefoot.

5. Meeting with others around our kitchen table to read poetry and listen to music.

6. Hearing my wife singing (it means she's happy).

7. Writing an article that touches others.

8. Music.

9. An English meadow in springtime ...

"If all these were gifts that God gives," writes Ann Voskamp, as she looks back over the start of a list that never really ends up ending, "then wasn't my writing down the list like... receiving? Like taking with thanks?"

And this is what she concludes, by the way: that in giving thanks for the life she had, she began to discover the life she'd always wanted.

Here is treasure. The simplest things we really love, made a little more evident, celebrated for what they are, received with appreciation, and brought fully into the realm of What Matters Most.

You could start your own list. And see where it takes you. You might notice that in giving thanks for the life you have, you can discover the life you always wanted. It's a mystery. And What Matters Most will not be the same for you as it is for me. But discerning what you love, and therefore What Matters Most to you, will help you to see how you have been created to be, and who you have been created to be, and what God loves especially about the way you have been created to be... Which is, after all, unique. For in bumping into God, and in discerning what we love, and in understanding how we've been made... we also bump into ourselves, sometimes as if for the first time.

11

Love wants to be known

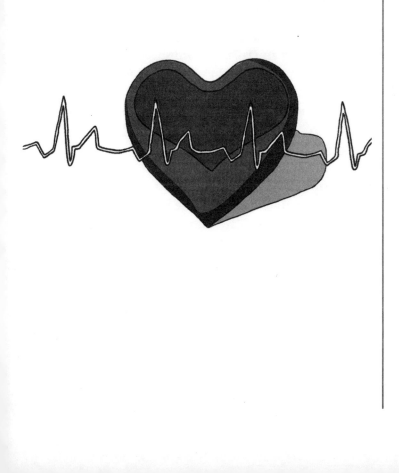

Have you noticed how whenever we stop to count our blessings, a different kind of emotional and spiritual space opens up before us, around us, and within us? It's as if we begin to see the world afresh, and feel the presence of goodness surrounding us and lifting us and inspiring us.

Why do we feel moved when we experience goodness and beauty? Why do we feel inspired by the sight of clouds, oceans, rainbows, sunsets? Why do we feel restored and renewed by experiencing forgiveness, or by receiving help, or by accepting support or by hearing encouragement? Could it be that Love itself is reaching out to us, drawing us inexorably closer to What Matters Most in the end?

The theologian Dallas Willard suggests that "love always wants to be known". It seeks to make contact. It seeks to transform us. Love wants to be known, and is stretching out its hand to cross the divide. Love *loves* to be known.

Love matters

And love, of course, matters. We know it, instinctively.

If you've been to a wedding service in a church, the chances are the reading was taken from that famous passage written by the apostle Paul (in 1 Corinthians 13), which so eloquently speaks of love. "Love is patient, love is kind. It does not envy, it does not boast…" It's a very moving passage, which seems to touch people profoundly, of all faiths and none. It expresses *something* more of the ineffable nature of Love.

Whatever we do, Paul suggests – if we do it without love, we are nothing, and we gain nothing. Even if we are experts in religion. Even if we give all our money to the poor. Our actions will count for nothing. They will be lost. What we do without love will not last. I don't believe that's a threat – it's a wonderful encouragement to remember that life is not always as it seems, and that this seemingly intangible thing we call "love" is the vital ingredient within all that we do, as we try to live freely and creatively and to play our part lovingly within this changing world.

I think we know this, deeper down, even if we haven't yet stopped to articulate it: that the greatest challenge and opportunity we face, above all, is to live as if love matters most in the end.

That's what my friend John has decided. "I believe the answer is Love," he wrote to me, in the conclusion to his poignant correspondence. "I see it clearly, and I deeply desire to live in it…

"I have come to see that love is goodwill," he continues. "It means willing that good will come to another person, or yourself. Out of that come all our actions, or our choosing not to act at all."

As we set down our egocentric desires, and find our places within the goodness of God's creation, then we can allow Love itself – which reaches out to us – to flow through us, to the world around us, and to guide our way.

As John concludes ultimately, "It is Love that loves well."

Ashes or Gold

In a beautifully haunting song called "Ashes or Gold",
the singer-songwriter Miriam Jones imagines a day of
reckoning, when our lives are finally sifted.

When the promised fire falls
on our heads and on everything we know,
it shall be made plain, the worth of it all:
burned to ashes or refined to gold.

When my life is repossessed
and the truth shines her light into the hold,
all I have done, cursed and blessed
will burn to ashes or be refined to gold.

Her words issue a great challenge to me. What will
remain of what I have done, and who I have been? And
by what measure shall my life be judged? If I value love
more than anything, perhaps it's obvious that I should
expect it to be judged against the measure of love itself.

You may have, or have nothing at all
but in the end all the homeless will come home,
and where your heart is, what you've loved above all –
will burn to ashes or be refined to gold.

When we come to look back upon our lives – in fact,
as we do so *even now* – there will be dross, of course:
things we've done or achieved or bought that, in the
end, will seem utterly insignificant, and which find
no place in the Unguessed Picture, even though at the
time they may have looked so valuable.

Yet there'll be other things too – perhaps
surprisingly – that will stand the test of time, and

which – looking back, now – prevail, *simply*
because they were motivated by, or infused with,
or embodied, love itself.

Death is the greatest change agent

The knowledge that we will, one day, die, must
surely help us to focus – if we face it – on what is
truly important to us in the end.

In his memorable speech at Stanford University
in 2005, the man who co-founded Apple, Steve
Jobs, spoke poignantly of death, having been
diagnosed with a very rare form of cancer. He
knew, at that point, that he had won a reprieve
(in the end, he died in 2012) – but he spoke with
the clarity of a man who had stared death in the
whites of its eyes.

"Remembering that I'll be dead soon," he told
the students graduating that day, "is the most
important tool I've ever encountered to help
me make the big choices in life. Because almost
everything — all external expectations, all pride,
all fear of embarrassment or failure – these things
just fall away in the face of death, leaving only
what is truly important."

Leaving only what is truly important.

What now? Three quick ideas

1. A reality check

The leadership expert Tony Schwartz suggests that
58 per cent of people say there are significant gaps
between what they say is important in their life

and how they actually live. (And perhaps the other 42 per cent are being kind to themselves.)

You can test yourself on this by asking how much the different areas of your life matter – and he suggests the specific categories of:

work/career,

financial success,

your spouse/partner,

your children,

wider family,

friends,

fitness,

your faith,

creativity and self-expression,

your happiness,

learning and growth,

and service to others.

Write down a score out of 10 for each of these categories (as well as for any other areas you can think of), depending on how important they are to you. Now ask yourself how you'd rate (out of 10) the *quality of energy* you give to each of those areas. Subtract this score from the first, for each category.

If you have a score of zero for any given area, it means you're aligned; you're giving the requisite energy and you're living pretty well as if you mean it. If you don't, it's worth noticing which areas of your life have the greatest gaps between what you *say* is important and what you give your energy to. (A score of 2 or over is particularly worth paying attention to.)

How can you close the gap between what you say matters and the way you live your life? What steps can you take to give a higher-quality energy to what matters more? What might prevent you from living with integrity? And what can help you to start living as if What Matters Most really does matter most while you still can?

2. Find a rhythm to life

As you begin to see what is truly important to you, it's crucial to build habits and rituals into everyday life in order to create rhythms that allow you to flow more freely with What Matters Most to you. Otherwise, this will have been an academic exercise, in which we thought some nice thoughts about love and life, and nothing more.

None of us can do what we specifically want to be doing every moment of every day (though we can learn to approach each moment or phase of the day with an appreciative attitude, in order to look for what's good, lasting, and loving within the whole of life!). But we can make sure that we make space in our lives for what is truly important.

We tend to work in four shorter-term rhythms – the rhythm of a day, a week, a month, and a year – and it's helpful to break our lives down into these rhythms so that we can take small steps to ensure each part of our lives becomes a microcosm for the whole, in a positive way.

There could be some things you feel are crucial to do every now and again – such as to take a holiday, for example. You can't do this every day, week, or month – but you might feel it's vital to do this every year.

So try to reflect, very simply, on what *one thing* matters so much within each of those four shorter-term rhythms – the day, the week, the month, and the year – that you make sure you do it.

Start with a **day**. Having read this book, what one thing do you feel you must have done by the close of every day? It might be to pray or meditate. It might be to spend quality time with your family. It might be to have worked well on a project you love. Or to have undertaken manual work or gardening. (You don't have to restrict your list to one thing, but one is a start. Try not to make it too long a list, whatever you do, as you won't end up sticking to it. Clear and simple will help you to achieve your daily goal.) For me, it's to make sure I give myself a short period of time each day for silence and prayerful contemplation.

Now, the **week**. What do you wish to ensure you have done across the course of a week? (This, for me, is where my running comes in. I aim to run at least three times during the week, because I know it keeps me fit and gives me significant times of creative breakthrough.) Perhaps for you, it's meeting a friend, or taking a long walk, or watching a quality film, or playing sport...

Then there's the **month**. What is it that you should not let a month pass without doing if you are being true to what you value highly and what's most important? Perhaps you'd like to factor in an element of personal retreat (taking one afternoon a month for reflection and regaining perspective). Perhaps it's to do with serving in your community as a volunteer. It might be to do with a hobby – making sure you paint a picture, or create something with your hands, or go sailing, or whatever it is that brings you alive.

And then, the **year**... A holiday? An annual decluttering? A course to learn something new? A visit to distant relatives? What is it that matters most for you across the course of a whole year?

Hopefully, then, you will end up sensing very clearly what is truly important in terms of maintaining a good, loving, and lasting rhythm to the whole of your life. And you will be able to hold yourself accountable for living in a way that demonstrates to the rest of the world exactly What Matters Most to you.

3. Make a stop-doing list

This sounds like it could be negative, but the leadership guru Jim Collins, in his book *Good to Great*, is positively adamant that if we wish to flourish, then we should know precisely what it is we must *stop* doing as much as knowing what we should start...

So you might like to make a stop-doing list and keep it in your diary or journal alongside your other reflections. I'm very clear about mine: I want to stop "surfing" with my phone in front of my children, and I want to stop being distracted by emails when I'm working. I want to watch less TV, and eat less junk between 9 p.m. and 10 p.m. (my weakest time!).

What could you stop doing that will help you to start doing more of what is most important to you?

*　　*　　*

In a recent reality-TV experiment called *The Island*, the survival expert Bear Grylls sent a group of British men to a remote island to see if they could manage to find shelter, water, and food enough to stay there for a whole month. They were successful, and as you can imagine, the experience felt deeply significant for most of the men. They had become disentangled from the ephemera of today's culture and had been able to reflect for themselves sharply upon What Matters Most.

One of the group reflected poignantly, at the very end, how he had tasted something of what life was really about. "I don't want to spend the rest of my life just keeping up with emails," he said, sighing.

And so say all of us.

And so say all of us.

A final reflection:

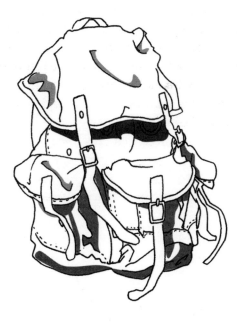

Committing to the adventure

Back when it was possible (and some might say even fashionable!) to sneak into the Glastonbury Festival without paying, a couple of hard-up friends of mine used to "go over the top" – scaling the great fence that stood between them and a whole new world... But the only way to do it was to throw their rucksacks over first, at which point there was no going back.

I'm not certain they'd ever read the Scottish mountaineer William Murray, but he'd have been proud. The only way to fully commit to the journey ahead, he argues in *The Scottish Himalayan Expedition*, is to throw your knapsack over the wall. Then you have no choice but to go after it, and keep on going.

"Until one is committed, there is hesitancy," he writes, "the chance to draw back; always ineffectiveness. Concerning all acts of initiative (and creation) there is one elementary truth, the ignorance of which kills countless ideas and splendid plans: that the moment one definitely commits oneself, then providence moves, too. All sorts of things occur to help one that would not otherwise have occurred..."

Have you ever noticed that? It's *when* we commit, that providence, serendipity, Spirit, Life, can really start to move.

"Boldness has magic in it," says Murray.

I pray you be bold.

Works mentioned in the text

Brother Andrew with John and Elizabeth Sherrill, *God's Smuggler*, USA: Penguin, 1964.

Rob Bell, *What We Talk About When We Talk About God*, London: Collins, 2013.

Andrew Bienkowski and Mary Akers, *One Life to Give: A Path to Finding Yourself by Helping Others*, New York: The Experiment, 2010.

Cynthia Bourgeault, *Centering Prayer and Inner Awakening*, Cambridge, Massachusetts: Cowley Publications, 2004.

"Regina Brett's 45 Life Lessons and 5 to Grow On" can be found on Regina Brett's website: http://www.reginabrett.com/life_lessons.php

Brené Brown, *The Gifts of Imperfection: Let Go of Who You Think You're Supposed to Be and Embrace Who You Are*, Center City, Minnesota: Hazelden Information & Educational Services, 2010.

Barbara Brown Taylor, *An Altar in the World: Finding the Sacred Beneath Our Feet*, Norwich: Canterbury Press, 2009.

Frederick Buechner, *Now and Then: A Memoir of Vocation*, San Francisco: Harper & Row, 1983.

Shane Claiborne, "13 Hopes for 2013" – http://www.redletterchristians.org/13-hopes-for-2013/ The community of which Shane is a part is called The Simple Way, and its website is http://www.thesimpleway.org/

Jim Collins, *Good to Great: Why some companies make the leap… and others don't*, London: Random House Business, 2001.

Agnes De Mille, *Martha: The Life And Work Of Martha Graham*, New York: Random House, 1991.

Annie Dillard, *Pilgrim at Tinker Creek*, Norwich: Canterbury Press, 2011.

Pope Francis, *Evangelii Gaudium: 231–232*; given in St Peter's, Rome, 24th November 2013.

Jaco J. Hamman, *A Play-Full Life: Slowing Down and Seeking Peace*, Cleveland, Ohio: The Pilgrim Press, 2011.

Transcribed notes from a Jaco Hamman lecture on hope can be found on a blog by David Dark, *Peer Pressure is Forever* – titled "Wishing and Hoping": http://davidsarahdark.blogspot.co.uk/2014_03_01_archive.html

"Ashes or Gold" is taken from Miriam Jones's self-published album *Fire-lives*, available at http://miriamjones.bandcamp.com/album/fire-lives

Tobias Jones, *Utopian Dreams: In Search of a Good Life*, London: Faber & Faber, 2008.

"Let Yourself" by Martyn Joseph is taken from the
    album *Songs for the Coming Home* (Pipe Records,
    2012). Further details about Martyn's charity
    Let Yourself Trust can be found at http://www.
    martynjoseph.net/let-yourself-trust

John O'Donohue, *To Bless the Space Between Us: A
    Book of Blessings*, New York: Doubleday, 2008.

"Sometimes" is from Sheenagh Pugh, *Selected
    Poems*, Bridgend: Seren, 1990.

Richard Rohr, *Immortal Diamond: the search for our
    true self*, London: SPCK, 2013.

Tony Schwartz, *Be Excellent At Anything: Four
    Changes to Get More Out of Work and Life*,
    London: Simon & Schuster Ltd, 2011.

Anna Swir, "To That Which is Most Important",
    reprinted in *Soul Food: Nourishing Poems for
    Starved Minds*, ed. Neil Astley and Pamela
    Robertson-Pearce, Northumberland: Bloodaxe
    Books, 2007.

Dave Tomlinson, *How to be a Bad Christian: …
    and a Better Human Being*, London: Hodder &
    Stoughton, 2012.

Ann Voskamp, *One Thousand Gifts: A Dare to
    Live Fully Right Where You Are*, Grand Rapids,
    Michigan: Zondervan, 2011.

Bronnie Ware, *The Top 5 Regrets of the Dying*,
    Alexandria, New South Wales: Hay House,
    2012. For more information about Bronnie
    Ware and *The Top 5 Regrets of the Dying*, visit
    hayhouse.com.au or bronnieware.com

Dallas Willard, *The Divine Conspiracy: Rediscovering Our Hidden Life in God*, New York: William Collins, 1998.

For more information on Brian Draper's work, visit www.briandraper.org